THE
GAME UNTOLD

By: Tyrus R. Brown (Tucker)

The Game Untold
Copyright © 2014 by Instant Publishing
All rights reserved

Published by: Instant Publishing
Printed in the United States

Book Designed by Michael Washington

No part of this book may reproduced or transmitted in any for or by any means, electronic or mechanical, including photocopying, recording, or by any information storage and retrieval system, without permission in writing from the publisher. The publication is designed to provide accurate and authoritative information in regard to the subject matter covered. It is sold with the understanding that the Publisher is not engaged in rendering legal, accounting, or other professional services. If legal advice or other expert assistance, the services of a competent professional person should be sought.

ISBN Number: 978-0-692-26645-8

By: Tyrus R. Brown (Tucker)

Tuck

Email: 901tucker@gmail.com

Instagram: @tuck_901

Instagram: @tuc901

Twitter: @tuck901

Table of Contents

ACKNOWLEDGMENTS 7

CHAPTER 1: THE EXCHANGE
PART 1 9
PART 2 13
PART 3 17

CHAPTER 2: THE CHASE
PART 1 27
PART 2 45
PART 3 61

CHAPTER 3: THE OPTIONS OF THE CHASE
PROLOGUE 87
PART 1 91
PART 2 101
PART 3 107

CHAPTER 4: HIDDEN SECRETS 111

CHAPTER 5: THE DECISION
PROLOGUE 143
PART 1 147
PART 2 151
PART 3 157

CONCLUDING THOUGHTS 161

ABOUT AUTHOR 163

Acknowledgments

I would like to first thank my number one supporter God for giving me the patience and will to write this book. I thank my beautiful mother Debra R. Tucker (Smith) and my second mother Maria Hunter. I thank my father James W. Smith for being a good role model. I thank my brothers, Lloyd W. Tucker and Denzelle C. Tucker as well as my oldest sister Britney E. Tucker and my baby sister Destiny Smith. I would also like to thank my grandmother Margret Tucker for her support and grace. Without my core family I would not have the insight and knowledge to even write.

    Thank you. I thank my close friends and brothers, Ervin Mitchell, Quenell Williams, Cameron Allen, Greg Moore, and LaQuan Carter. I also thank Katrina Muldrow, Sherri Scott and everyone in the admissions, records, and financial aid offices at Southwest Community College for helping me and always being there. I thank Michael Washington and Wanisha Lyon for supporting me and helping me edit this book. Also Randrica Hopper and Laquita Britton and the numerous other people who have helped me reach this point in life past and present. Thank you. Without you, I would have never been able to write this book. Anything is possible and because of you I have been able to make one of my dreams and become reality. I love you all.

The Exchange

PART 1

When one thinks of exchange, you think of the definition; an act of giving one thing and receiving another. That's exactly what happens when the not so average, not so typical guy meets three different women. His name is Eli, an extremely successful doctor and owner of many real estate properties which he has inquired over the years. He doesn't have any kids and his bank account contains over six figures. He's a very head strong leader that is known around the city.

    Eli has three degrees along with his PhD. Yes! He is not the average Joe but he has been the average Joe before. He's a great catch right? I know what you're thinking. Eli, has to be gay or on the crazy side because he seems to be perfect. Well, he is not gay and Eli is only crazy about his mother. Although Eli and his mother share a great relationship, he never knew his father but never dwelled on the thought of it. Some women get the misconception when a guy seem too perfect or have great things going for themselves; they instantly associate it with something negative. This could be vice versa. Imagine if he was just a good guy, I'm aware they come slim to none nowadays but sometimes you can push a good person away based on personal past experiences. Okay! Eli is lacking in the height department but Eli is very muscular and attractive. Eli appeals to the eyes of a lot of women.

Eli's personality is very outgoing, loud, and fun, but his flaws include a lack of patience. Sometimes Eli might come off as overly confident. This causes some to perceive him as arrogant or cocky based on his outer appearance. Eli is aware of this misconception. However, over the years it has improved. Now Eli is at a stage in his life where he knows women inside and out. So he plays the role, feels them out, dissects their mind, and analyzes them to see what their true intentions are. Eli is past the stages where he manipulated, and controlled thoughts of women, making them feel a certain way. Now, he sits back and observes the individual that is best for him. Now, let's get started!

The first chapter is called the exchange: breaking down the exchange of the acts that started it all. Eli meets three different women roughly around the same time but in different locations. Part 1, talks about lady number 1, known as the gold-digger. This will be the first lady Eli will encounter. Eli met her around 11pm at the jumping new hot spot, Senses, a night club in Memphis, TN. It is a typical night in the lime-life. Guys are being overly thirsty trying to approach every different woman that appeals to their eye.

Which many times, the encounter turns out to be negative because they have bad intentions. Eli notices lady number 1 dancing with her friends and she has his nose wide open and his full undivided attention because of her revealing clothes. She has a spaghetti strap top enhancing her breasts so they can sit up neatly. This see through skirt is equipped with the latest red bottom heels in order to set off the entire ensemble. She has red lipstick soaked around her plump lips and is wearing a Juicy Couture necklace.

Let's just say he can appreciate her God given curves and her individual sense of taste and flavor. Most clubs are very loud. Different varieties of music are played such as hip hop, R&B, soul blues, country, reggae, and pop. My point is that Eli really cannot converse with her because there are too many distractions. It is just not the right scene. The first thing Eli does is analyze his prey. He makes his observations and waits patiently to proceed. It has to be the right time and moment to approach her.

When her friends are done dancing and the song is coming to a close, he makes eye contact and taps her gently on the shoulder to get her attention. He notices through subtle gestures that she is analyzing him. With refreshing breath, he approaches her correctly, not pulling her, nor yelling at her. He looks her directly in her eyes letting her know he is engaged in the conversation that they are having, despite the interrupted scene.

Eli asks her a few simple questions including her name, what she does for a living, if she is single, if she has any children, and if she is in some type of school. Her response is, "Do you have a job? If so, where do you work and what can you do for me?" Totally disregarding what Eli has to say, she gets straight to the point of what she is looking for. Eli instantly feels a bad vibe yet he goes along with the flow because he is still attracted to her. In spite of what her intentions are, he still has intentions of his own. So he just plays the game along with her, responding, "Yes, I do." She immediately tells him to take her number. Gladly accepting it, he tells her that he will call or text her the following day.

He then walks away with a feeling of accomplishment and a smile on his face. He thinks to himself, there has to be a story behind all this even though she is simply a gold digger. After his few moments with lady number 1, he can tell that she isn't trying to get to know him for the right reasons and she just wants to know what is in his wallet. Eli immediately puts her in the category of no good or just someone temporary to occupy his time. A person will never know the expectations of another person or be able to predict longevity when they meet.

They usually just go with the flow and allow things to develop. Eli becomes curious of knowing every possibility of her including those attributes she may not even know that she possesses. However, he still wants to sleep with her while in the process Eli is thinking that learning about her truly will eventually allow him to build some type of interest. He could possibly fall for her and really start to gain true respect for her. It is still very early and he can't make this justification because he simply does not know what the future holds with lady number 1.

The Exchange

PART 2

The next lady Eli encounters is lady number 2. He meets her at the local mall in Memphis, TN. This mall is fairly busy at times but he is getting an outfit to go on a hot date with the "gold-digger" he had previously met at Club Senses. He sees lady number 2 at Macy's looking for shoes. Eli thought to himself, women love shoes, so they could be all day looking for a certain type. At that moment he noticed he had time to run around and get his outfit together and approach her. Thinking about beautiful lady number 2 that appeals to him with his naked eye, he goes to Dillard's and gets some Levi slim fit jeans, a burgundy blazer that compliments his jeans, and he already has a few shirts he hasn't worn at the house so he is good to go.

Looking real spiffy, Eli immediately rushes back over to Macy's but lady number 2 had vanished. He becomes very disappointed so he begins to walk toward the exit. Getting ready to leave the crowded mall, he sees her on her way to her vehicle. A bundle of joy comes upon him as if it is the Holy Ghost itself. She is so far from him that he thinks about giving up and walking the other way, but then suddenly out of nowhere she slips and falls. Her

Gucci slippers fell on the other side of the concrete, and all of her items fell on the ground. Rising up, Eli is there giving her a helping hand with a concerned look on his face asking, "Are you ok?" She quickly says, "Yes I'm okay now since you, the super hero, came to rescue me." He smiles and continues the conversation with a few jokes making her laugh numerous times.

    He notices she is dressed very conservatively yet still sexy and comfortable. He notices that she is not wearing any makeup and that her hair is slightly tied up. Eli asks her questions including her name, what she does for a living, if she is single, if she has any children, and if she is in some type of school. She replies to all of his questions bluntly with a soft smile. She asks him the same questions with a nonchalant smirk and he replies to her with joy.

    The connection and spark is amazing and they are clicking on every level, but is it too good to be true? She shortly announces to Eli that she has a boyfriend and that they are having a few problems in their relationship. However, she tells Eli to take her number because she doesn't mind getting to know him better. Eli, being the gentlemen that he is, carries her bags to the car to get a few extra brownie points and tells her that when he gets to his destination he will give her a call. She replies with an appealing smile, "I'll be looking forward to your call."

    He stood there for a moment to soak everything in and replies, "It will be a pleasure." walking away as if he hit the lottery, completely disregarding his date later that night. As he is walking down the street to his off white CLK 500 convertible Benz, he has all these thoughts going through his head. She had made such a big impact and first impression. He knew from the very start she was a keeper. He didn't know what the future would hold and Eli was eager to know what flaws he would encounter later dealing with lady number 2, also known as the naïve good girl. Leaving the parking lot, he comes to a red light with a smile. He calls her just to tell her he is thinking about her at that very moment and then tells her goodbye. He then tosses his phone into the passenger seat and drives to Starbucks to get a Frappuccino Cream.

The Exchange

PART 3

Eli later goes home and sees that he is low on groceries so he drives to the local Kroger to get a few items to fill his depressed refrigerator. It is a normal day at the local Kroger near his home. The lines are fairly congested and he is ready to leave. Time is winding down until his hot date with the "gold digger." Eli goes to the meat section trying to find some seafood but he can't find the brand he is looking for. He is gradually growing frustrated so he thinks about leaving and heading to the Wal-Mart that is approximately 25 minutes away. Eli suddenly realizes that he doesn't want to waste his gas nor his time so he simply decides to do without and deal with the circumstances.

    Proceeding to get the rest of his groceries, he positions toward the bread section and he sees this tall, beautiful, long-legged woman looking like a goddess from the gates of heaven. Immediately she catches his eye through her appearance alone. Once again, Eli analyzes his prey. He notices that she is tired and he can sense that she has a lot on her mind. He doesn't want to come on too strong. She is dressed fairly sexy. He notices that she has a passion mark under her lower neck that reflects against her dull cubic zirconia earrings. This lets Eli know right off the bat that she is sexually engaged with someone else. Eli is curious to know if she is single or available. Still amazed by her long frame, he doesn't know what to expect.

    This causes him to become even more interested in knowing things about her that lie deeper than what the naked eye can see. He approaches her and walks beside her slowly as if he is looking for the exact same thing that she is looking for. He tries not to make eye contact so that it won't be obvious that he is trying to talk to her. Finally he makes a gesture. He asks, "What types of bread are you looking for?" She replies, "The cheapest kind." Eli laughs and then says, "I don't blame you. This recession is no joke." With a smirk across his face he tells her his name and asks her a few questions as he did with the previous ladies he came into contact with.

    He asks her name, what she does for a living, if she is single, if she has any kids, and if she is in some type of school. She hesitates as if she does not want to answer the questions. She only answers the questions she feels most comfortable with. Thinking to himself, Eli wonders if the questions were really that hard to answer. In his eyes they were fairly simple questions that anyone could answer.

    Eli senses that her guard is up like most women but he continues to look her directly in her eyes as she continues. Out of no-where, this small, seemingly bad, kid brushes against Eli's foot to get to his mom who is apparently the lady Eli Is having conversation with. He thinks to himself, "She has kids?" but he never bothers to bring it up. The kid is screaming at his mother yelling,

THE EXCHANGE: PART 3

"I want a candy bar!" Suddenly the mom takes her hand which is slightly bent and smacks the child telling him to stop screaming in public. Eli stands there in complete shock yet he says nothing until she is done talking with her child. He feels that it isn't his place to speak on it or say anything because he has only known the lady for a few minutes.

Her beauty causes him to disregard what happened. Eli still attempts to get her number and succeeds. Eli tells her that he has a busy day ahead but that he will call her when he gets free. She told him, "its cool baby, call me. I'm on your time. I'll be ready when you need me." He walks away as if he has had sex with her already but thought to him- self that this was too easy. There is more to this story. He was intrigued seeing what the future held between the two of them but in the back of his head he knew it would not be long.

He could sense it. However, love has a way of sneaking up on you when you least expect it. It was the flow of the mind game he would later pursue. Eli met three different types of women all in the same week and he was feeling on top of the world, yet deep down inside he was lonely and unhappy. He had only been in love one time.

The one and only love of his life had broken his heart so deeply that he didn't think he could ever fall so intensely in love like that again, but he knew that he loved the feeling of being in love. This feeling that took over his mind and gave him hope of a better day when he had bad days. He longed for that desire to give his all and build an empire and not just a relation- ship with that special individual. However, a lot of these women were so broken from all their previous relationships. Most women have countless amounts of heartbreaks under their belt.

They seem to have a tendency to build a wall to keep away anyone they feel is trying to get too close because they were afraid of being allowed in that place where they were vulnerable, naïve, and blind because there heart was so deeply engaged within the other person. A woman is naturally emotional. She tends to wear her heart and feelings on her shoulders and she forms a wall to protect herself.

All the guys that once had her attention and heart took a certain degree of piece, joy, and innocence so she is hard on anyone that tries to seek her trust. One's trust is hard to gain and very few people will receive it but all women seek completion and this fulfillment of love security. They all desire this deep within. Most women tend to let their guards down at random times for a guy that they feel may have potential. On the other hand, down the line, they regret it because now they are dealing with another heart break and time is wasted.

That's the main reason why a woman is cautious. Women get tired of being in certain situations and dealing with the same thing over and over again. That outlook changes their way of thinking and how they interact with guys in general. Some build certain personality traits based on things that happened to them in their past. The gold digger seeks financial stability; therefore, the gold digger will perhaps leave you if you lose your ability to provide for her financially. A good person can appreciate your financial resources but a gold digger appreciates only that and will not see the relationship as worthwhile if you're not well off.

They feel that they deserve to be treated well and that includes knowing that someone is willing to spend money on them. Maybe it's because they have had a bad childhood or relationship and they feel they deserve to be happy and it just so happens that their joy carries a high price tag. Maybe they feel it is their right to be able to pursue their big dreams at the expense of financial stability and coincidentally, they have not considered who will foot the bill of their soul searching.

Have you noticed unreasonable expectations of especially favorable treatment? This sense of entitlement is one of the symptoms of narcissistic behavior which is just one of the symptoms that a potential gold digger might harbor. Now take the innocent naïve girl, she tends to believe people at face value. She has frequently been burned in friendships due to people taking advantage of her extremely warm and giving nature.

She is also sexually inexperienced and has extreme difficulty fulfilling the sexual desires a male wants fulfilled. In ways these women will likely be very loyal in a marriage to a man that they love, I think the innocence and never "getting it", would eventually overwhelm her positive qualities. The funny thing is that often times these women may hold decent jobs and have a lot of book smarts but they won't have some of the most basic street smarts. They have often been very sheltered growing up and this carries over into their adult relationships.

Another aspect of a woman being naïve and innocent is that often times she will act immature and childish as well. Usually the naivety is a symptom of a larger immaturity problem that can manifest itself in many different ways. They often don't have the emotional maturity needed to be in a healthy relationship. Lastly, take the good girl gone bad girl concept; she was broken so many times by so many different guys, her mind was reprogrammed not to have feelings or emotions so she won't have to go through the pain of always getting hurt and let down. She feels as if this is the best method to cope with situations that happened to her throughout life.

    The good girl that is turned into a bad girl is labeled as a whore in most societies because she won't allow herself to feel. Yet it's always a story behind everything that hits the surfaces. She seeks love in all the wrong places, she tells herself she would allow someone to capture something so valuable from her; however, they will respect her and value her. She gets content with being the side option because she needs someone to vent out to. Someone that will love her when she feels she doesn't love herself that day or moment.

    Maybe she was brought up never having a father like structure to teach her to value her body and peace of mind. Maybe she didn't have that close bond with her mother because they were so much alike that they couldn't get along at times. So she then seeks understanding, affection, and happiness from all the wrong guys yet, feels that they care for her and love her. This being the only way she knows because she has been doing this for so long and she starts to accept the ideal of being a whore in society. She feels the only way she can get a guy's attention is from her body not her mind. She even experimented with being with the same sex to see if it was just the male race.

Although her feelings with women were much intimate and closer with a lot of emotional roller coaster rides unexpectedly because they are the same sex. Women are emotional creatures of course, and they will crash eventually. The sweet, innocent small girl is lost in this big world and she accepts what she has become. However, deep within a great sadness and pain suffocating her thoughts and mind, she longs for a better relationship with her mother and she longs for a better respect for herself. It's like she's in a hole but simply can't get out of these dark feelings.

Her past haunts her as if she sees no real future, yet the very moment she does, her acts of taking different women and men results in her acceptance of the mistress role. Meaning, not having any type of feelings only caring and thinking of herself and watching the other women feel pain as she once did when she was the naïve lost girl that simply wanted to be loved. She made the decision not to care anymore with no remorse with the different actions she displays.

She continues to do what she does, breaking hearts and never having feelings. She was first a sweet good girl, now, a ruthless bad girl that has no feelings at all and doesn't believe in the word we call love. She is incapable of being alone. She always finds a way to feel that she is wanted and needed. Some result too sleeping around and others will just jump into a new relationship right away. However, the same can go for guys. It's just less noticed because it's more socially acceptable for guys too sleep around than it is for girls. It's far too easy for a girl which is not the same for a guy. Although we think it is easy, it's the process of getting back on the horse and being able to communicate while working the situation out.

Make the move and finally seal the deal. It creates confidence which heals. Women really have no need for this process specifically if they are attractive. So, by women going out and screwing some guy it doesn't hold the same level of merit as if a guy does it. For a guy to actually be able to do it, he needs to be strong and confident. A woman doesn't usually want to get laid, she just needs to go up to some guy and say "Sex?" and that, itself is destructive. Something that comes so easy for a girl will only breed thoughts of low self-respect. She'll focus on the fact that she has no self-control.

The second point is, guys have the ability to have sex and not attach emotions. For a girl, sex to them always seems to mean something. Therefore, the process of getting a lay will only add to the emotional crap they are contending with already. Guys, just the way we are made can avoid this. Men are logical and women are emotional at times. One night stands usually result in the girl feeling used. A guy trying to heal a woman with a broken heart that still sleeps around will be destructive. Having to talk to so many different women and learning them over a course of years gets played out because the chase was simply a game and the game will eventually die when one thinks of the thrill of the chase.

Part of seduction or looking for a partner is the sheer enjoyment of the chase. Many instances of male and female interactions are enjoying the chase and actually wanting to be caught sooner or later. Men have to have a chance to chase and conquer in real life situations. The inner man demands the chase. So what does the man do once he 'has his prey' especially after he has had a chance to munch on it for a while? He moves on to the next chase. The experience of the chase is what's important, not reaching the goal.

The relationship between efforts and values are so closely associated in a consumer's mind that they would want the best outcomes automatically which results in increased preference for any outcomes associated with efforts, even pointless efforts.

The Chase

PART 1

Eli is finally at his lavish penthouse bachelor pad after leaving the local Kroger's. As he placed his groceries on the floor, he looked at his watch and realized he had only 2 hours left until his hot date with lady number 1, the gold digger. He quickly put the groceries up, and pulled his iPhone out that had most of his smooth R & B music. He played some old school R.Kelly and ran his warm water to start his shower. He was 30 minutes in the shower when he heard a noise; it was a phone call from lady number 2, the naive good girl he recently met at the mall.

    He jumps out the shower, naked body shivering, smelling like his dove for men body wash to get the ringing phone. He answers, hello, and lady number 2 starts to speak. She asks him what he is doing. He tells her, "You might not believe me but I just ran out of the shower rushing to get the phone." She laughs and says I have something to tell you. She tells him that her and her boyfriend haven't talked or seen each other in two days. She is becoming worried and she wants some advice. She feels embarrassed because they have just met but she has a burning desire to know what she was doing wrong in the equation. Eli listens to what she has to say but suddenly notices time is winding down for his date. He doesn't want to be late for his date, but he is a gentleman so, he at least acknowledges what she has to say and gives her some small feedback.

He tells her that they could have lunch and they could talk about it tomorrow. Eli gets off the phone with her and proceeds to get ready for his date. He puts his new, navy blue, Levi slim jeans on and his blazer to compliment them. He brushes his hair, puts his diamond earrings in, and sprays his Playboy London cologne. Eli has chosen to take lady number 1 to Olive Garden and he has to go pick her up. He calls her to ask for the address to her house and she quickly tells him that she lives in Cordova near the mall.

When he arrives, he finds himself in front of this big house trimmed in baby blue layers with reddish bricks. The yard is clean and the bushes are neat. He notices that she has two luxury cars sitting out Front. She has the latest Porsche and a CLK 320 Benz in all black. Eli is very impressed and curious to know what she really does for a living. From the first conversation at the Club, she never gave him any information. She only appeared to be concerned with what he did for a living and how he could help her out.

Eli had all these questions in his head about what she actually does for a living. He calls her and tells her that he is outside. She tells him to come in because she isn't quite ready yet. Obviously she doesn't want to be rude by allowing him to wait on her outside and burn gas. Eli thinks to himself, that it was very considerate. He agrees and then knocks on the door. He notices that she has big doors as if she is a queen of some sort. She opens the door wearing nothing but a robe with this sweet scent that draws Eli's body closer to her. Eli can feel a warm sensation under his legs but he quickly gets his mind off the illusions of knowing and wondering.

    He has a seat on her all white sofas that wraps around the living room. He makes himself more comfortable because he knows that he may be there for a while. She walks to the back of the house to finish getting ready. He begins to observe the house. While sitting down his head is spinning back and forth looking around at her nice works of art. He figures that she must have money based on the qualities surrounding him. He figures out that the house has 8 rooms including a living room, game room, and a 4 car garage.

    He waits there patiently for about 25 minutes when finally she arrives wearing this beautiful dress that is half unzipped. She asks him if he could help her zip her dress up. He quickly gets up and proceeds. He can smell a sweet, soft, scent laid upon her warm, soft, skin. As Eli pulls the zipper up, his hands gradually caress her Shoulder. He uses this to balance the weight of his hands. He slowly zips her dress up. She replies thanks you in a way that implies that she has him wrapped around her fingertips.

    On their way out the house a car pulls up. It was another luxurious car, the latest 2014 Lexus. The windows were dim so Eli couldn't really see who was in the car. Walking away from him she moves towards the car. He is trying his best to see who is in the car but he simply cannot. As she leaves the mysterious car, Eli notices an older white man in the vehicle. He doesn't ask questions he just gets into the car and drives with her to their destination. They are late for their reservation but she has some type of connection.

Clearly she has been there a lot because everyone from the workers to the manger knows her. They received the best table and they finally got settled in. They both browse over the menu even though Eli isn't really that hungry anymore since he had to wait so long for her to get dressed. She is clearly hungry or just eats a lot because it seemed like she ordered the entire menu plus some. Eli got a small plate of Chicken Alfredo and to top it off, a Brandy Alexander. She ordered three Walk Me Downs, a huge plate of Chicken Alfredo, and a few side dishes.

The food finally arrived and they begin to eat. A few minutes into the rest of the evening and they had time to get a few more drinks in their systems. He then makes his way into getting to know her, making her smile to loosen the setting. So he begins to ask her a few questions. First he asks, "Who was that guy that came over to your house earlier?" She replies, "That was a friend of mine.

We have known each other for a few years now." Eli felt it wasn't his place to get deeper into that so he left it alone. Eli also asks her what she does for a living and she replies, "I'm a lawyer with my own law firm and I have recently gone through a bad divorce with a cheating husband." There he had it; this explains everything about the way she came off at him when she first met him. She was hurt and broken because the man she had been with since she was 16 years of age cheated on her. Her husband had a baby outside their marriage with a younger lady.

She married him when she was only 19. Eli thinks to himself, that's too young to get married in most cases. It just depends on the person and their maturity level.

Marrying young is not a bad thing if you are ready for it. He suggests you shouldn't marry young because of wanting a baby before turning 30 or because you've been dating someone for a long time and it just seems like the natural progression is easier than breaking up. Marriage is about being able to commit to someone when life is shitty and when life is good. It's about not always getting your way and having another voice in the conversation that is just as important as yours. It can be about raising a family too if that's what you decided as a couple.

The two choices are not "get married and live happily ever after", or "bar hop your way through the better part of your child bearing years and regret it for the rest of your life." We all are well acquainted with the divorce rate and we don't want it to be us. Add a postgraduate education to a college degree and toss in a visible amount of career success and a healthy helping of wealth.

Now let it simmer in a pan of sexual variety for several years, allow cooling and settling, then serving. Since we are young, our generation has been advised by parents, teachers, and after school specials to focus on our careers, our independence, and ourselves and the rest will fall into place but this is certainly not how things actually work in reality. Getting back to the passage, lady number 1 discusses her ex-husband's child's mother explaining that she is not very attractive. Eli laughs as she proceeds. She explains that she tried taking him back after he hurt her so deeply. She at least attempted to make it work because he was her husband after all, not just a boyfriend or a man she picked up off the streets. She said the real reason they started having problems was because of long distance.

He had gotten relocated to a job 5 hours away permanently. The pay was good but the distance was extremely far. She had to ask herself how they could make it work. He waits to give her feedback and shortly replies, "The first part of a long distance relationship is deciding what you want. Are you willing to do what it takes for this person?" You may want it to work with this person but before you start a journey, know what it is going to take to get to the finish line.

A lot of long term relationships don't work because one or both people can't take it. It is just too hard for them to do so. Long distance relationships are not for everyone. It is up to the person to decide whether or not it is for them. It is important to know why you are doing it. Hopefully, it's not just because of momentary benefits. If you're in it for the right person, always know why the person is worth it. Remember what it is that you like about them, what made you decide they were worth it all.

Sometimes it just doesn't work because two people are not meant to be but a lot of times it doesn't work because people forget why they do the things they do. Everything relies on communication. This is one thing that can end any relationship, not just a long distance one. Somewhere along the line, couples stop talking to each other. That's the worst thing that could ever happen. People need to talk to share their emotions and their feelings. It's what keeps the sparks connected. Without communication you just have bodies and people that are just going through the emotions without having any true meaning. Don't go days without calling or at least chatting over the internet.

People respond better to seeing someone or hearing their voice. Texting alone will not stand for communication between times. Trust can be a big issue with people but the truth is what we make it. Either we don't trust our partner or our partner doesn't trust us. We have made trust become a problem. You can avoid these problems. It's as simple as not creating a situation where your trust can be compromised. Let your partner know that they can trust you. Trust is what a person makes of it. The big key to making a long distance relationship work is simply patience.

The best things come to those who have patience and wait. The end result is much better than the time spent apart. It may not seem like it now but it will become clearer one day. With long distance relationships time seems to be a big issue but patience is the one thing you have to make it work. Try to see each other as much as possible. The longer the time apart, the more likely of a split, if you can make it happen, do it. Even if you have to cancel plans be sure that you make time for one another.

Sometimes, the spur of the moment does us all some good. Every relationship has their fights. The thing is if they can't be avoided, but pick them wisely. When your partner is there you can fight with them in person but long distance fights tend to be more brutal. Not in a physical way, but in a more emotional way because words that are said are taken more seriously. Silent treatments aren't the same. Everything you say and do, are ten times worse than if you were actually face to face. This can lead to events that neither one of you really want. If you have to fight make sure it's something worth fighting over. It can easily be the little things that blow up that end it all just because one of you picked the wrong fight. This can be hard for a lot of people.

Having voids or needs that you expect to be met and things that may be small and unnoticeable that somehow mean more. Things like someone to sleep with every night, someone to be there to comfort you when you're down. Things that we generally want the one we love to do when they are with us. Learn that being in a long distance relationship you will have to make some sacrifices. Meaning you have to give up things some times to get better things in the future. Don't try to find other people to fill those voids.

It seems as if when times get rough people start looking for others who can fill their emptiness but you have to understand that being in a long distance relationship includes your voids not being met every day. It seems that when two people who know so much about each other don't see each other every day, grow further apart. Their lives are lived differently. They start to adjust to their new surroundings and turn to the people that are currently in their lives.

The best way to avoid this is to share everything. Every person you meet, every new thing you try, share it with your partner. Showing your partner how much of your life you want to share with them whether or not it is something good or bad. It lets your partner know that you're not trying to hide anything and you want them to be there every step of the way. After Eli shares his insights on her and her husband, she is very impressed by how smart he is.

She listened and made her own observation based on the information he had given her about long distance relationship but her trust would not allow her to forgive him because she was torn by the hurt and pain. They would argue about senseless, petty things. She accused him a lot of sleeping with his baby momma. Her marriage was going downhill. She asked Eli what he would do if he were in the situation. Eli replies, "First I would concentrate on myself; redeeming the mistakes I have made and ask God to show me how to change, rather than concentrating on the failures of my partner.

Don't blame yourself or let others blame you for choices that your husband is making. Recognize that you can't change your husband, so don't try to reform him. Don't nag or scream. That's not going to make you any more attractive to him. He will just use it to point the blame on you. Changing your husband is God's task. The hardest time may be when you are reconciled and you have a tendency to fall back into your old habits. Lastly, if your husband leaves you for another woman and then returns, don't expect your husband to change overnight. It takes time to allow yourself to trust him again piece by piece.

It's hard at first but pray about it and remember communication is key. Tell him how you feel other than just yelling and building an argument because that will get you nowhere but where you started." Eli knows that she is fragile and has serious trust issues. She was hurt and cold and held a wall up so high that it was extremely hard to bring down. So she played men, took from them, and used them. It was because she was at stage where she was tired of getting hurt.

She developed a concept of not gaining feelings and taking advantage of guys, manipulating them with her beauty and persuasive ways to get exactly what she wanted. She never wanted to feel used or played again. For years she played men and took from them. She was the average gold digger, but there was a story behind why she did what she did. Like most women it's a story behind the smile and the silent cries. She used her charm like a man to take control of the situations because she felt that all men wanted was sex. She made them work for what she had to offer but in most cases she never slept with them.

The chase was real and clear. She would get numbers from guys and never call or save them and would forget she even met them if they were not talking the same language. Deep within she was hurting and longing for something that is real. All the success she had gained over the years meant nothing because she didn't have anybody to share it with. After a while she grew tired of using men. She just wanted someone to give her love, affection, and attention. She really didn't want their money anymore because she could finance and provide for herself.

She just needed someone to genuinely understand her, to love her through her wounds and flaws, and be that missing piece she longed for after she was heartbroken by a man she thought she loved and could trust. Eli observed certain traits as he was talking with her. She didn't have to say much, but certain things she implied told him the rest of the story. Eli asks her what her favorite color is in order to cut the tension in half so she doesn't have to relive the painful thoughts again. She is now totally engaged in the conversation and is really feeling him because most guys she comes in contact with wouldn't want to know about her past.

He pushed the painful memories out and made her truly express herself like no other. She grew to respect him more as the conversation unfolded. She judged Eli based on her previous experiences with guys, but the more and more she talked with Eli, she felt a piece of her growing and glowing. It was a great feeling, something she hadn't felt in a while. He knew that a woman couldn't be a gold digger and seek love forever. She would have to give up one or the other.

Eli knew that she was starting to be an open book as the night proceeded. In his younger days, Eli was an average typical young guy and all he wanted was sex and to build his number count. He played the game hard, fast, and senseless with no remorse. Most women desire to know what makes a guy just want sex and nothing else. The answer is that he is finding things out about himself as a young man. He was once hurt before, but didn't know how to handle his mixed emotions. Growing up as a young man, they are taught to show no weakness and be a man.

Eli told himself he never wanted to get attached nor feel loved or seek love over the course of years. Eli would eventually grow out of this immature stage of a having a small boy's mind frame because eventually everyone needs love and something real. He couldn't play the game forever because the game would eventually play him back in return. Any woman that feels comfortable with a guy will naturally open up to him; specifically if she has had sexual chemistries and mental chemistries with him.

They may even have spiritual Connections. Once a spiritual connection is made then it's pretty much a done deal. A person can get anything in which they desire. The game is that a woman wants to be chased. That shows her that you care but the chase will only last for so long, until eventually it plays out. Never allow a guy to chase you for too long because the guy's only focus will be to have sex with you and move on. You have to make him chase you, yet give him something to desire. It could be, learning more about you or giving him more affection, which doesn't include sleeping with him right off the bat.

Most of the time when women give themselves up so easily. It's because they spend a lot of time with a person or text them on a regular bases and that causes her to think he deserves the goods, which is most likely not the case. Most women eventually come out saying he doesn't treat me how he used to. This is because he already got the goods so he has no reason to treat you like he used to. Yet if you make him wait too long for the goods, a guy will lose interest. However, he still wants to get the goods even though he has lost all true interest due to being forced to wait.

Once he gets what he wants sooner or later he'll disappoint you by ending what you have because you made him wait too long. So there's no such thing as giving it up too soon because too soon to you could be too late for him. It has to be the right timing in the midst of two people truly getting to know each other. You can't get to know a person through a text message or going on a few dates, which is what most women think. It may take years to truly know a person.

Most people that have been married for years don't know their partner completely. You can never truly know a person unless you experience failure and over- come that failure. That's how people in relationships build history and a solid foundation of true genuine love. You would think a couple that has been together for 50 years or more wouldn't have any failures or break ups and make ups but this is not always true. Love can never be defined and most people try to figure the construct.

Love can cheat on you at any time. Some people in relation- ships that love their partner unconditionally also think about cheating. Eli fully understands the concept and tries explaining it to his date. Getting back to the evening; the night is almost over and Eli and his date are both full and have had a great conversation. Now it was time to leave. Surprisingly, she pays the bill unhesitant.

He didn't get a chance to say he would pay for it, which is a sign that she is a strong woman that's willing to pay for the bill. It's usually the other way around. Most women are traditional, meaning in most cases they would look forward to the guy paying for the meal. I agree with that but if you feel there is chemistry like no other, then do something different that guys are not used to and I promise you this will stand out to him. You won't be compared to the average female. It's the small things we tend to look over that do the trick every time. While Eli and his date had a great evening, it was finally time for him to escort her home. On the way to her house they resumed their conversation. She asks him if he has ever been in love and he tells her that he has.

Eli also explains that he was heartbroken. He even went a bit further telling her he was a dog as well. Eli explained how he would sleep with countless amounts of women, but over the years he just seemed to grow lonely and tired of doing the same thing. He explains that he's now at a stage in his life where he's not forcing the issue. He is allowing it to come to him and he has been honest about everything from the beginning of any relationship or friendship he has encountered. She never had a man to tell her the raw truth.

Most men will try to lie and shockingly she knew parts of their game but not the full game so she was somewhat shocked. She really respected him and felt she could trust him already because he had been so honest and respectful. Finally they arrive at her house. He tells her that he really enjoyed the evening and hopes they could keep their friendship going. She asks if he wants to come in and have a few more drinks. Eli smiles and tells her no because it is getting late.

She smiles and tells him thank you with a wink. She tells him to text her when he makes it home safely. He waits until she is in the house safely then he drives off quickly. His thoughts were racing. This was unexpected because he had viewed her differently the night at the club. His respect level for her had completely changed.

THE CHASE: PART 1

It was eight minutes of him driving and he thought to Himself, "We are grown. We make our own decisions and rules so why not end the night off right?" He goes to the local grocery near her house and gets some chocolate covered strawberries and some roses then drives back to her house. She is singing all around her place with joy and fulfillment when she notices his car was back in her drive way. She is so surprised! Maybe she had left something and he was being a gentleman and bringing it back to her.

She is already undressed and the house is dim. Keith Sweat's music is playing in the background. She puts her robe on and proceeds to the door, and there Eli is. He grabs her, and gives her a graceful hug and then tells her, "I brought these for you, if you would like, we can both treat each other to a meal," she smiles and says, "of course, but you have to eat me first," and winks at him. He closes the door firmly and the magic begins. She offers him a portion.

She takes a glass from her home bar and places the roses he got her around her master bedroom. The lights are dim and the mood is just right for anything to take place. She goes back in the room where Eli is located and sits around the area he is sitting and enjoys the wine. They talk and flirt and both of them know how the night will end. They are just enjoying the thrill and desire of the chase. He asks her if she is feeling kind of tense and offers to give her a massage.

He slowly takes her robe off and begins to rub her back intensely with slow, strong, hard motions as if she is the last woman on earth. Her hormones are raging and she is beginning to get this warm tingle around her inner thigh, which runs through her spine up to her collarbone. She is ready for whatever is in store. Eli is a gentleman. He doesn't rush the situation but instead he allows it to come to him. He is now feeling this sensation he can't control any longer. It is at its' highest peak. As he rubs her back, he gives her a soft kiss in the middle of her spine that sends shivers up and down her spinal cord.

  He firmly grabs her waist and begins to lay her down. Taking off her robe completely, he is amazed by how well her body is put together. Eli sees that there was some ice around the area. He takes the ice out and places it in his mouth and begins to lick around her breasts. She is in shock but it feels so good, she continues to let him do as he pleases. At this point they are completely naked. They have passionate sex knocking things over all around the house.

  They eventually end up in the shower with her back against the wall and the water pouring down on both of them. The back of her hair begins to curl up as the water hits it. Her hair gets soaking wet as he pleasures her up and down against the hard wall. Her eyes roll back to the back of her head. She begins to moan louder but, it eventually gets to a point where she can't moan any more. They are finally done after a few hours, both drained and lifeless.

  They lay in the bed naked and peaceful. They are wrapped around each other very tightly, lying in each other's juices, and looking into each other eyes till their eyes begin to dim. They sleep for a few hours and then Eli gets a text in the middle of the night that wakes him up. He begins to put his clothes on and gives her a gentle kiss on her forehead. He tells her he will text her when he makes it home safely.

The Chase

PART 2

The night is still young but Eli is drained. Once he gets out the shower he rolls over in his king size bed and begins to rest his eyes. Luckily, he doesn't have to work the following day. He just sleeps and lounges around until he receives a text message from lady number 2 better known as the naïve good girl. He had forgotten they had plans that day. She asked him what he had planned around 3:30. He looks at the time. It is roughly around 1:47 pm. He then replies, "Nothing, just hanging out with you." She replies with a smile and tells him to meet her at the local IHOP on Union Avenue.

    He gets off the phone with her and begins to look for an outfit. He thinks a simple vest outfit will do for their meet up. Eli arrives at the IHOP early to get a good table. She comes a few minute late as he expects. She walks in the door, not knowing where to go. Eli politely calls her over and tells her that he is at the far right corner waiting on her. Eli notices that she is dressed very comfortable yet still sexy while not revealing too much. She is wearing a light blue jacket because she knows it will be chilly in the restaurant.

    She is also wearing a green sundress with pink

flowers going across the bottom. She finally sits down where he is sitting and they begin to crack a few jokes and flirt the day away. She begins to get deeper in the conversation because she has a lot of mixed emotions passing through her head that she feels she needs to vent out and release. Eli is deep in thought while staring her directly in her face listening to everything she has to say.

    Eli pays close attention to her body movements and gestures. She is very passionate and very into every word she is saying. She begins to express and explain her feelings. She explains to him that she has been talking with a guy for over 11 years. She is emotionally drained and damaged over the toxic relationship. She says that he cheated on her and talks very badly to her but she feels as though she can't leave him because they have so much history together.

    She knows he cheats but, she doesn't want to face the reality of him saying he cheated because she has been with him for so long. She is comfortable and that's all she knows at this point. She doesn't want to start over with anyone new because she feels it will be a long process of building that familiarity so; she remains content with her situation. She would rather listen to his lies in order to cover up the hurt and pain that she tries to ignore. Women go through stages where they are just wild and just basically exploring life.

    They later get to a point where hanging out grows old and tiring so they begin to want to settle down with this ideal type of guy. Once women get this guy they think desire them, they later realize that he is usually not what they need. Now they feel kind of stuck in a place where they are confused and are left basically trying to find their way and figure themselves out. Then they take a break from guys because they are trying to figure out what they want to do with themselves. She implied that her boyfriend is her everything. Although, he was very controlling and didn't want her to have friends or talk to her family.

All these things have taken place and she is still crazy for him. Maybe it is because he is her first and only. She begins to tell Eli how her boyfriend pressured her into having sex with him. She was a virgin and she didn't really know what sex was but, she was very curious of the subject. She couldn't talk to her mother about sex because they weren't really close on that level. She knew if she were to talk to her mother about sex; her mother would judge her or eventually they would get into an argument, so they never had the conversation. The guy she was dealing with knew she was naïve.

He was a few years older than her and he was more experienced than she was. Most of her friends were engaging in sex. It was the norm. When you're in an environment where everybody in your age group is doing something you are likely to conform to the situation. A person may hear friends talk about their sexual experiences and what sexual things they have done but that does not mean that you have to do the same. You may not even be sure that they are telling the truth. Plus, everybody is different and we all have different comfort levels.

Just because you are attracted to someone and want to be sexually intimate with them that does not mean that you have to want to do 'everything' with them sexually. What you do with someone is not a sign of how much you like or love them. However, it is a sign of respecting each other and your decision is a sign of his or her love or respect for the relationship. She tells Eli that the first time her and her boyfriend did it she really didn't want to but it was like a mental thing.

She felt that if she didn't have sex with him at that moment, then she would lose him. She said no at first but they were already naked and he was kissing on her. He was trying to stick it in but she was too tight so he began to rub on her spot to loosen her up. She began to push him away slightly but her body gestures were singing another tune. It's like she wanted it but she didn't because she was scared and nervous.

He placed the tip in and she tried to stop him but he kept going and she began to like it, so she let him continue. She began to beg for it and would get mad when she couldn't have it. She was passive and emotionally unstable. Most would call it sprung. The old saying is: sex brings feelings, especially in a woman, because they have so much love to give. Women are emotional creatures, whereas men are more physical and have the ability to separate love and sex.

Most women are not going to have sex with just anyone if they have no attraction and feelings towards him. As for Men, we don't necessarily have to be attracted or feel love towards a woman to have sex. For most, outside of a committed relationship, it's just sex. Some men have a short attention span and pretty much stop thinking about the woman once they get what they want. They might think about her half an hour before the next attempt, but there are very few men who are constantly fantasize about an average encounter. Even though sex is supposed to be very hormonal and neurochemical, our perception of it is very different based on gender.

The bottom line is, if you don't want to have a full relationship, find someone who will be willing to just have casual sexual intercourse with you. Relationships like this usually don't work, however usually the woman starts feeling the other person in spite of having the limitations on the relationship. This always leaves one wanting more from the other. This is medically and scientifically shown. It's due to men having high levels of testosterone. Testosterone is located in the men's genitals and in the ovaries for women. Due to the high levels of testosterone in men, it's the likely cause for the urge of sex.

For men the spark usually ignites immediately to the reaction of sexual needs. As for women, the spark stays ignited for as long as much of the effect has taken on her. The word love, which most women desire at first causes them to get hurt so many times that they become afraid of the heartbreak that comes when the good situation becomes a bad situation. Most of the time it is more lust than love that people feel but most people confuse it because it feels like love in the beginning stages. In relationships, there is either lust or long-term attachment.

Lust is primarily physical and fleeting for both sexes but long-term attachments take years of shared experience to develop in either person. Women falling in love are mostly common in relationships. I recognize that women can experience something called love at first sight, but for a man it doesn't work that way. Love for a male is something that starts early and continues or it doesn't start at all.

A man judges his woman primarily in relation to himself. A woman evaluates her man on how he relates to the outside world and this takes longer. The important thing to realize is that you cannot expect less to make a man gradually fall in love with you in the same way that you might fall in love with a man.

Eli knows the type of guy she is describing based on the vivid information she provides. He shortly gives her feedback on what she might be dealing with. He tells her a controller has very shallow emotions and connections with others. One of the things that might attract you to a controller is how quickly he says, "I Love You," or wants to commit to you. Typically, in less than a few weeks you'll receive gifts, a variety of promises, and be showered with their attention and nice gestures.

This is where they catch you and convince you that they are the best thing that ever happened to you. Remember the business saying, "If it's too good to be true, it probably is too good to be true!" You may be so overwhelmed by this display of instant attraction, instant commitment, and instant planning for the future that you'll miss the major point and not notice that. Normal, healthy, individuals require a long process to develop a relationship because there is so much at stake.

Healthy individuals will wait for a lot of information before offering a commitment not in just a few weeks. It's true that we can become infatuated with others quickly but we should not make such unrealistic promises and have the future planned after a few weeks. The rapid warm up is always a sign of shallow emotions which later cause a controller to detach from you as quickly as they commit. A controller has a scary temper. If your boyfriend or girlfriend blows up and does dangerous things, like driving too fast because they're mad, breaking or throwing things, getting into fights, or threatening others; the anger will soon be aimed at you.

In the beginning of the relationship, you will be exposed to "witnessed violence", fights with others, threats toward others, and angry outbursts toward others, etc. You will also hear of violence in their life. You will see and witness your partners temper, throwing things, yelling, cursing, driving fast, hitting the walls, and kicking things. That quickly serves to intimidate you and cause you to fear their potential for violence.

Although, a controller quickly assures you that they are angry with others or other situations, and not angry with you. First, you will be assured that they will never direct the hostility and violence at you, but they are clearly letting you know that they have that ability and capability and that it might come your way. Later, you will fear challenging or confronting them, fearing that same temper and violence will be turned in your direction. People who control relationships constantly correct your slightest mistakes.

They try making you feel "on guard," unintelligent, and leaving you with the feeling that you are always doing something wrong. They tell you that you're too fat, too unattractive, or don't speak correctly or look well. This is gradually chipping away at your confidence and self-esteem and allows them to later treat you badly, as though you deserved it. In public, you will be "walking on eggshells" always fearing you are doing or saying something that will later create a temper outburst or verbal argument. The cycle starts when they are intentionally hurtful and mean.

You may be verbally abused, cursed, and threatened over something minor. Suddenly, the next day they become sweet, doing all those little things they did when you started dating. You hang on, hoping this means the sweet cycle is the last one. The other purpose of the mean cycle is to allow a controller to say very nasty things about you or those you care about, again chipping away at your self-esteem and self-confidence. A controller often apologizes but the damage to your self-esteem is already done, as planned.

A controller blames you for their anger as well as any other behavior that is incorrect. When they cheat on you, yell at you, treat you badly, damage your property, or embarrass you publicly, it's somehow your fault. For example, if you are ten minutes late for an arranged date, is it your fault that your partner drives 80 miles per hour, runs people off the road, and pouts the rest of the evening. No it is not, but that is exactly what they want you to think.

A controller may tell you that their anger and misbehavior would not have happened if you had not made some simple mistake. They also may say that you should love them more, or had not questioned their behavior. A controller never, I repeat "never," takes personal responsibility for their behavior; it's always the fault of someone else's. If a controller drives like a maniac and try's to pull an innocent driver off the highway to assault them; in the controllers' eyes, it's actually the other drivers fault for not using a turn signal when they changed lanes.

They give you the impression that you deserve the anger, the yelling, violence, pouting, or physical display of aggression. Controllers will lash out at you, call you names, or say cruel or embarrassing things about you in private or in front of people. When in public, you quickly learn that any opinion you express may cause them to verbally attack you, either at that specific time or later.

If you stay with the controller too long, you'll soon find yourself politely smiling, saying nothing, and holding on to their arm when in public. You'll also find yourself walking with your head down, fearful of seeing a friend who might speak to you and create an angry reaction in the presence of the controller. It's never enough: A Controller convinces you that you are never quite good enough. You don't say "I love you" enough, you don't stand close enough, you don't do enough for them after all their sacrifices. Your behavior always falls short of what is expected. This is another method of destroying your self-esteem and confidence.

After months of this technique, they begin telling you how lucky you are to have them. To have someone who tolerates someone as inadequate and worthless as you. People often let you know about their personality by the stories they tell about themselves. There's an old saying about giving a person enough rope and they'll hang themselves. The story a person tells informs us of how they see themselves, what they think is interesting, and what they think will impress you. A humorous individual will tell funny stories on himself. A controller tells stories of violence, aggression, being insensitive to others, and rejecting others.

They may tell you about past relationships and, in every case; they assure you that they were treated horribly despite how wonderful they were to that person. They brag about their temper and outbursts, because they don't see anything wrong with violence. They actually take pride in the "I don't take anything from no one" attitude. People define themselves with their stories, much like a culture is described by its folklore and legends. Listen to these stories they tell you how you will eventually be treated and what's coming your way. It's been said that when dating, the way an individual treats a waitress or other neutral person of the opposite sex is the way they will treat you in six months.

During the "honeymoon phase" of a relationship, you will be treated like a king or queen. However, during that time a Controller has not forgotten how he or she basically feels about the opposite sex. Waitresses, clerks, or other neutral individuals will be treated badly. If they are cheap, you'll never receive anything once the honeymoon is over.

If they whine, complain, criticize, and torment, that's how they'll treat you in six months. A mentally healthy person is consistent; they treat almost all people the same way all the time. If you find yourself dating a man who treats you like a queen and other females like dirt, hit the road. As mentioned earlier, mentally healthy individuals are consistent in their personality and their behavior. A controller may have two distinct reputations - a group of individuals who will give you glowing reports and a group that will warn you that they are serious trouble.

If you ask ten people about a new restaurant, five say it's wonderful and five say it's a hog pit. You clearly understand that there's some risk involved in eating there. A controller may actually brag about their reputation as a "butt kicker," "womanizer," "having a hot temper," or "being crazy." They may tell you stories where others have called them crazy or suggested that they receive professional help. Pay attention to the reputation. Reputation is the public perception of an individual's behavior. If the reputation has two sides, good and bad, your risk is high. Let's now resume the conversation they are having, Eli notices she is starting to tear up around her eyes and her makeup has started to run down her chin.

She states that her boyfriend is just different now. He isn't the sweet and genuine guy she fell deep in love with in the beginning. He has become another person but she feels as if she just can't let him go because he is all she has ever known. Even though they are having a lot problems, she sees him as her foundation. When he wants to be good, he can, just on his time. She continues to be his fool because they have so much built between one another, good and bad.

Despite this, she still wants the experience of communicating with another guy because it can be her way of exploring something different. I guess you can say she was still curious. She hadn't had experiences with other people because she wasn't allowed too. I feel every woman needs to experience different relationships in order to teach them what and what not to do. These different experiences are a part of growing and maturing either for self or when building a relationship. Most people are able to gain these experiences earlier in life while some others may never gain them.

Eli listens to her carefully paying close attention to the small details maintaining direct eye contact while she explains her situation. This makes her feel like he actually cares about her feelings and reassures her comfort zone. This causes her to continue pouring her heart out to a stranger she just met. Eli knows exactly what is going on. He doesn't reveal too much. He doesn't want to give up too much information too soon. Eli knows she is weak and vulnerable.

He could easily take advantage of her, but he is a gentlemen and respectful. Besides, he only views her as a friend because she came on too soon and too strong plus she's still in love with the wrong guy. She is very inexperienced and he simply can't create the vibe to take it to a serious level beyond that of just a good friend. He tells her to look at it this way. What if a man allows a woman to control him? Women can only control a man who allows himself to be controlled. Love does not mean giving up your friends or only talking to the friends she chooses for you to talk to.

It also doesn't mean she gets to make all of the decisions in your life. If you are a man being controlled and you can't see that you most likely need some serious help. Women who control their men are in a much larger power struggle within themselves than they are with the men they control. The man is not the issue and what he does right or wrong, assuming he does anything right, is also not the issue. The woman in this scenario must realize she has problems that need to be dealt with and controlling her man certainly doesn't need to be a part of the resolution. Again, as the man being controlled, you are allowing it. Stop already! If you are a man in this type of relationship and you think for one moment you're going to change her, you're sadly mistaken.

    She is the only one that can change herself. That is one decision she most certainly must make for herself. You will not find some magic potion to suddenly make her share the decision making with you. The problem is much, much deeper. Typically, a controlling woman breaks down a man's confidence little by little until the man begins to believe he is nothing without her. Controlling women are manipulative and intimidating. Controlling women are often so good at this that they make the man feel he is the one responsible for making her angry or upset.

    She may often accuse him of being uncaring or insensitive to her feelings. Often, the man begins to feel it was indeed all his fault. Many men with low self-esteem will continue to allow this to happen. Often, he will change his behavior to "keep the peace" or simply to escape the circumstances causing the current episode. Along with this, his self-esteem plummets even further. Controlling relationships tend to come in phases. Did she take your breath away? Did she sweep you off of your feet? Many times this is how it all begins. Then she will find small ways to be manipulative and break down your self-confidence. She can turn every conversation into something that the man has done, such as being uncaring or hurting her feelings.

Suddenly, he finds himself completely in love with this control freak and wants to believe the woman that swept him off of his feet will return. Sadly enough, without some serious intervention, that most likely will never happen. In all relationships, there are leaders and there are followers. For the most part, that's quite healthy. However, when the woman spends most of her energy trying to control her man, she needs to look deep within herself and find out where this issue comes from.

These women must learn to understand that you can't gain control of your own life by controlling others. You can only gain control on your own life by controlling yourself. Until the controlling women face this fact and deal with it, they will not change. These types of women will continue to prey upon those men with low enough self-esteem to suck them into their controlling way of life.

They will continue to feed on these men for as long as they will allow it. Getting back to where they left off. Eli notices that they have been talking for hours. He could feel her comfort level rising based on her actions and her choice of words. He immediately put her in the friend zone because he knew she had a lot to learn about life. She was extremely naive on all levels.

She had a lot of potential but needed a lot of work. If a guy see's potential in you, he may be willing to be patient. Some guys lack patience and if you don't already have yourself together mentally, physically, and spiritually then they might just pass you by for the next candidate. In life you realize timing is everything and what you invest in someone you create a better outcome and even better results. In the middle of their conversation she gets several text messages from her boyfriend but she is so engaged in the conversation that she never replies. She simply views them and proceeds with the conversation. She shortly receives a call from her boyfriend. With rage and frustration, he asks her why she did not return his text messages. She tells him that she is out with a friend. He hangs up and she bursts into tears.

    Eli tries to calm her down but it is too late. She tells him that she has to go. She says that she will talk to him another time. She then rushes out of IHOP leaving her food that she barely touched and her gold MK watch behind. Eli was in disbelief. He was already very tired and this situation made him even sleepier. He pays the waiter and asks for a take-out plate. He rushes home to get some rest because his body and mind is on overload. He is able to sleep for about four hours until he wakes up. Then he brushes his teeth, jumps in the shower, and is finally able to let his body and mind get the rest that they deserve. It is now 8 o'clock in the evening.

The Chase

PART 3

Eli decides to call the good girl gone bad girl that he met at the Kroger. The phone rings but there is no answer, so he waits patiently for her to answer the phone. She finally calls him a few minutes after he called her. He answers, "Were playing phone tag I see. This is the guy you met at Kroger that other day, Eli." It was a moment of silence at first then she said, "Who are you again? I don't remember. "Eli says, "Your kid ran over my foot while we were talking in the middle of Kroger looking for bread and I asked you a few questions as well." She said "Oh, I remember you now. Hey boo. How are you doing?" He responded saying he was okay and he had had a long couple of days. She immediately asks when they could see each other. She was so direct and blunt and Eli liked the fact that she was straight to the point.

    She didn't sugar coat anything or play hard to get as most women tend to do in the beginning stages. Playing hard-to-get implies some degree of push and pull. She has to make you want to "get" her in order for her to make getting her "hard." Unless you are too forward early on, this usually means she has to show a sign of interest or two. Look for all signs of interest, but especially the subconscious ones twirling hair, nervous tics, strong eye contact, mimicking body movements, open positions. They're harder for them to control and will reveal more. Be careful. Attractive women will often flirt with guys they have no interest in for a variety of reasons. The cause could be anything from getting free drinks to simply stroking their ego.

Some are experts at selling their attractiveness to guys and will do their best to get the most out of it. Be suspicious if things that come a little too easily. Dating is often like a game and the players have different tricks up their sleeve. Women have grown up with the advice not to be too easy to get and not to make the first move, "Smile at him, but don't talk to him first.", "Don't be too nice and don't ask for his number.", "Don't jump and agree for a date." "Say you are busy this weekend say maybe next weekend. "These are the rules that mothers have passed on to their daughters. This is the traditional way of thinking. Of course these rules have changed and now it is up to individual choice to stick to which rules they like.

Some men are dumbfounded by these rules. They are confused when the girl refuses a date. Some may back out at once, thinking the girl is not interested but these guys do not have any understanding of the rules of the game. The girl may just be playing hard-to-get in order to enhance the thrill of the chase. This game of hard-to-get may work initially, but it may lose its' spark in the long term. The guy will now be convinced that the girl is definitely not interested if she persists with this "Catch me if you can" game for long. Sometimes the guy thinks, "Forget her, she doesn't like me." The girl must give some indication that she is interested, for the game to work. Sometimes playing hard-to-get backfires. Most people prefer honesty and avoid game playing. They like to be able to put things clearly in their minds. People play games when they are not looking for a committed relationship or when they are convinced that you are not the right one for them. So don't chase after an obstinate case of hard to get.

Women who do this think that playing hard to get makes the men crazier about them. They may hand out dates as favors but such girls will not usually succeed in their romantic life. On the other hand you have men who will not take no for an answer. Playing hard to get is not completely evil. In a small dose, it can increase the level of excitement in a relationship. Give your love interest enough to want more but also preserve an aura of mystery about yourself.

Don't throw yourself all over him. Have some activities planned that do not involve him. Keep some space between the two of you. This will keep the romance thriving. Men are interested in women who are selective in their romantic life. They are choosy about their mates. It is a boost to their ego that they are involved with such a woman. If a woman is playing hard to get you need to not give up immediately but persist for a while in the game until you are convinced she really does not fancy you.

If she is totally not interested, you will notice she has short responses and pays more attention to other people. These certain signs of disinterest can't necessarily be "reversed" with a reciprocal sign of interest. In some cases if a woman comes on too strong, a man will think she is easy or possibly even undesirable. Then again he can think she is strong and knows what she wants and goes after what she wants. It just depends on the person and their perspective. But getting back to the passage, Eli explains to his third date that he is on chill today and he really doesn't want to go anywhere because he is exhausted from the previous night.

So Eli asks if he they can just get some hot wings and meet at her place. She tells him that will be no problem but it would have to be after 12pm. She had to put all three of her kids to bed before he came over. She also said she didn't like bringing different men to see her kids, just out of respect. He totally agrees and respects the circumstances. He then tells her he will be over at 12:01 pm with a smirk on his face. She said cool. She tells him to have her wings hot in a very sexy kind of way. She then tells him that she will talk to him later. Eli lies back down for a few moments.

He receives a random text message from the gold digger. The gold digger stated that she had a wonderful night last night and everything was so unexpected but all worth it. All Eli can do is smile and blush over the phone. She asks him when they will hang out again and he replies saying very soon. He knows he has her wrapped around his fingertips but he doesn't want to come on too strong or too willing so he keeps his cool. He stays on the phone with her for an hour or two just enjoying the text conversation and the flirtatious chatter. He can tell she is really into him, but at this point he doesn't know how to feel about this situation. He tells her that they can resume the

THE CHASE: PART 3

conversation later. He looks on his dresser at the brown and navy clock. It is roughly 11:37. Eli jumps out the bed giving his back a long stretch and bend.

He notices that he really doesn't have any clean clothes because he had forgotten to take his clothes to the cleaners a few days ago. He races to the shower using his favorite smell good, dove for men. It is something about that smell that women love. He starts singing as if he can actually sing while washing his masculine body. He later dries off and puts a white 100 percent cotton V-neck over his back, something simple, black Adidas, and gym pants that are very comfortable.

He doesn't want to put anything too dressy because he doesn't want to make it seem as he is trying too hard. Eli texts her and notifies her that he will be running a tad bit late. She replies as if she already knew he would and asks Eli if he just wanted to meet another time. He quickly responds tonight will be fine. She laughs and tells him to get his ass over here then. Eli kindly tells her to send her address so he can GPS it. She is about 26 minutes away from him. She lives across town in an urban inner city project. He is highly cautious at first, but he is a man of his word so he types in her address and continues to be on his way.

It is late and Eli begins to realize there aren't any hot wings places open at the time. His only option is ordering pizza so he decides to grab Papa Johns and he also decides to grab a Red Box movie. He prefers something scary. He finally arrives at her place. It is a two bedroom duplex and it is a fairly, modern home. The grass is not cut and Eli notices a few toys in the yard. He rings the doorbell and as she is walking towards the door she is wearing a long t-shirt that comes all the way down to her knees. She has this smell to her that is very rich and sweet that makes him rub his nose. It is quit refreshing.

    The kids are sound asleep in the next room so her and Eli sit on the sofa and begin to talk. He notices the passion mark on her neck is slightly gone. They begin to flirt and tell each other about themselves. Eli notices all the awards on the wall. He asks her how and what she did to receive the awards and she simply replies. "When I was younger I was very interested in sports and involved with school events but a lot of things got my mind off the important things I loved. It's complicated" Eli knows she is starting to get uncomfortable based on how she is starting to change so he gets off that subject and starts to talk about himself.

    Eli opens up to her explaining his relationship status, which is single. He said that he can't find anyone worth his time and effort and currently he is just mingling and keeping his options open till someone sweeps his mind, body, and soul off the ground. She laughs and tells him "You're very deep." Eli laughs, replying, "Something like that," and then asks her if she is single. She tells him that it's complicated which lets him know that she is talking to someone. She says they are having problems in their relationship signifying she is interested in Eli so she didn't want to run him away which is why she uses complicated as a safe route.

    He has no problem with her remarks because as he stated earlier, they are just mingling and there is nothing wrong with two single people just mingling. Eli notices

THE CHASE: PART 3

she has a lot of pain inside. So much that he can just feel it. He knows there is a story behind her. He asks her if she has anything to drink and she replies "I may have some juice in the fridge." Eli says that he is looking for something to loosen him up a bit. She smiles "I got something that will loosen you up," pulling out some old Jack Daniels. Eli exclaims, "You like brown liquor don't you! She said "I like whatever gets the job done but in my opinion clear liquor is much better. Brown just goes down easier." She gives him a few shots and she also takes a few herself.

    He tells her that he wants to know more about her to try not to hold anything back. She looks at him like he is crazy but she slowly starts to open up. She begins explaining that her relationship with her mom was very complicated. She says she had a rough time growing up because her mom was in and out of her life. Her mom was on drugs heavy for the large part of her life. She states that her dad was around but he went to jail for robbery when she was about 5. He was released from jail when she was 9. Telling this story caused her to get emotional. Eli has become so engaged in the conversation that he cannot not drop his eyes away from her.

    Her eyes begin to water as she tells him about how her father and how he used to touch her when she was younger and it soon turned into intercourse when she reached the age of 13. Her sperm donor told her he would kill her if she ever told anyone and it escalated to a point where she had to give her father oral and have sex with him. She felt ashamed, shocked, and used blaming herself because she was afraid to tell anybody. She just didn't know how her family would respond. Her father was the only person that raised her due to the fact that her mom was in and out of her life ` because of her drug problem.

  He would buy her anything she wanted. She loved him even though it was sort of a strange relationship. On one chilly and sunny day, she invited her friend over whom attended school with her just to spend time with her talking about cute boys at the local school and working on their project. They were doing a project for school together and she walked to the store alone to get some supplies.

  She soon returned and when she got inside the house, her friend was acting different, and she was crying. She asked her what was the matter and her friend wouldn't say anything. She noticed that she had a fresh bruise on the top right of her arm so she asked her how it happened. She lied and said she fell so they resumed back to the school project. Days after all this took place, her other friends approached her while at school with anger and explained to her what had really gone on between her friend and her father that day.

  She sadly stated that her father was touching against her and later raped her. She was in disbelief at first but she finally came to the realization that her friend was seriously raped by her father. She was angry and upset and a few days later she finally built up the courage to confront her dad. He told her to stop listening to what others had to say. She stormed into her room and began to cry. A few hours later she told him she was going to tell the family what was taking place. The father told her if she was to mention anything that he would kill her. He then pulled out a gun and placed it in front of her face.

Over the years she had several abortions for her father and this caused her be destroyed psychologically. She later told her mother everything.

The sad part about it was that her mother did not believe her. She tried telling her aunt but she did not believe her either so she started to distance herself away from her family. Her father never raped her again after that day. Years passed and her relationship with her family was never the same. She started to get love from different older men to get the warm love she always de- sired.

A part of her knew that what she was doing was wrong but this feeling was like a drug because the moments she spent with the different men were what she needed at the time. She would drink and do heavy drugs to get her mind ready for the different acts she was exposing herself to. She felt a great sadness deep within but she was in denial. She then began to explain that later in her life, she was raped by a man she thought was her close friend.

He took advantage of her while she was drunk but she never told anyone because of what happened with the last situation. She became pregnant and she was couldn't decide if she should abort the baby or keep it. She made the decision to keep it. After this she became bitter and cold. Her trust level for men had vanished. She used men and took from them. She had no remorse after sleeping with them and erasing them. She was a man in a woman's body. She slept with men and women. She used to travel to different events to make money that she gave to a friend of hers that played the role of her pimp.

This pimp would beat her and occasionally force

her to have sex with him and other guys. She would set men and women up after they had sex with them. She felt she was a devil just living life in a human's body. Her faith in God began to weaken because she blamed him for all the bad things that occurred in her life. She felt if there was a God then why would he let all those bad things happen to her? She felt women were more emotionally attached and latched on to things at a faster rate. On the other hand guys where physically attached. She did this for years she was angry, cold, and confused about everything.

    She began to use drugs to ease the pain but when the high was gone the pain returned which resulted in her using heavier drugs to maintain her high so she wouldn't have to face the reality of her situation. She was a single mother that had to do what she had to do. She had been through hell and back yet she was beautiful on the surface and she was very intelligent and had street smarts. She learned the game the hard way in the streets. Having a child made her realize that she wasn't going to go back down that path of drugs. She told herself that enough was enough. She left her pimp and moved to another part of the city.

    She later got her GED and worked a 9 to5 at a local clothing store. She took online classes at a community college and graduated early with honors and later went to pursue her dreams as a nurse in the morning and a stripper at night. After hurting these men and taking their money she felt a crushing sadness. She was at a stage where she wanted true love and to happiness. She stopped stripping and started working at a local Walgreens as a pharmacy tech but she still had dreams of being a nurse.

One random day a tall, dark and handsome guy walked in the store and started making conversation. He was flirting with her the entire time but she wasn't paying him any attention. He asked for her number. She hesitated at first but she took a chance. She thought he was just another guy so she had her guard up initially but began to slowly like him after talking for a few months. They fell in love with each other and made two beautiful children, a girl and a boy. They were never married but they were together for 6 years.

A question women may ask in this situation often is: How do I know if he's just a procrastinator or if he really never plans to marry me? Since women usually mention marriage more quickly than men, it is not surprising that women find it hard to distinguish between a man who has cold feet and a man who will never marry them no matter how much time he is given. For a woman who has been doing some serious hinting about getting married, it could be hard to recognize that conversations about marriage have been replaced by begging and pleading.

Even smart, strong, women who are used to demanding rather than begging for what they want in all other aspects of life somehow fall into a trap when it comes to begging a man to marry them. Once you discover that you have been reduced to begging, it is time to move on. Not only does he not plan on marrying you but the type of guy who strings a woman along like this is likely to move on to more complex stalling tactics that can drag on for years without ever tying the knot. It sounds so mature and responsible for your guy to say that he will ask you to marry him as soon as "the timing is right," but this is just another stalling tactic.

Over the years we've heard all of the "it isn't the right time" excuses. They've ranged from men waiting for that big promotion to one man who wanted his brother to have enough time to grieve after his divorce before he was "forced" to participate in wedding festivities. People manage to tie the knot during less than perfect circumstances all the time. Nearly every member of the clergy has a story about a bride or groom who had to hobble down the aisle after breaking a leg or having a serious injury before their wedding.

Remember these couples when you're evaluating whether his reason for waiting really has any merit. Men who want to get married are men that propose. They don't try to find a way to delay things by recommending that you have a trial period of living together "just to make sure we're compatible." These are trial periods and they've all either left the relationship or are now many, many years into that trial period. Well the guy she was with finally asked her to marry him after 6 years and a few months.

Everything was great but there is one thing every married person will tell you and that is that marriage is hard. Anyone in the midst of that proverbial honeymoon period may have a hard time believing that, though. Those first few months after you tie the knot truly allow you to understand the notion of wedded bliss. Once life starts to settle in some inevitable problems crop up for most couples. We can barely even talk about budgets and expenses without getting all testy and defensive. There are a many problems that occur in marriages. It's kind of cliché, but he leaves his shit every- where! He never goes to our kids' school activities or plays.

Our marriage has three people; me, my husband, and his mother. Often we will "expect" the other person to do things in the way that we would have done it, be it showering the kids with attention or acknowledging a birthday or having dinner on the table after a particularly hard day. And when that doesn't happen, coming back from that disappointment is hard. We set ourselves up for it a lot of the time because maybe the other person didn't realize you wanted things done in a certain way or maybe our expectations are unfair and unrealistic.

He doesn't want any more kids, but I want just one more and figured this out a little too late, but I don't think we are actually sexually compatible. We don't spend enough alone time with each other. Between work, kids, and house stuff, I feel like I never see him. He doesn't help enough around the house. It's like he thinks the dishes miraculously wash themselves.

When I ask him to help out, he says that he's too tired. Like I'm not! We spend too much time together. I have no breathing room. He never tells me what he is thinking. It's like talking to a stone wall sometimes. He snores as loud as a freight train and won't do anything about it. He is obsessed with sports. He even tried to miss our child's birthday party because of some playoff game.

I'm like, what's more important here? He doesn't respect my career goals as much as his own. He spends way too much time at strip clubs and clubs period with his friends. He is Facebook friends with his ex-girlfriend. We never go on dates anymore. It's just work, home, work, and home. Where's the excitement in that? He's never around. Sometimes I feel like a single mom. We never have sex. It's like we are roommates. He never replaces the toilet paper roll. He will even open a package and use a new roll and just place it on the counter instead of in the holder.

There are break downs like this and every marriage has problems and situations that are hard to handle at times. Yet when you tie that knot to commitment through thick and thin it becomes your duty to handle your problems and save your marriage. If not, then your marriage will possibly fail like most American marriages do. The good girl gone bad girl's marriage failed mainly because her husband was verbally abusive and physically abusive which drained the life out of her.

A person may not recognize this eroding of their self-esteem and happiness through verbal, mental, emotional and other forms of abuse. A relationship can be unhealthy or abusive even without physical violence. Verbal abuse may not cause physical damage but it does cause emotional pain and scarring. It can also lead to physical violence if the relation- ship continues on the unhealthy path. Sometimes verbal abuse is so bad that you actually start believing what your partner says.

You begin to think you're stupid, ugly or fat. You agree that no one else would ever want to be in a relationship with you. Constantly being criticized and told you aren't good enough causes you to lose confidence and lower your self-esteem. As a result, you may start to blame yourself for your partner's abusive behavior. Emotional abuse is never your fault. In fact, your partner may just be trying to control or manipulate you into staying in the relationship. Furthermore, back to the passage, she just got tired of the dealing with the same stuff so she left the situation and moved back with her mother.

    Her and her mother had a better relationship even though they did not see eye to eye at times. She shortly found out her father committed suicide but she did not attend the funeral. She felt the main reason it took her ex-husband a long time to marry her was because he didn't forgive her for her past and he never fully trusted her. In the beginning their marriage was good but he would later step out on her and she kept taking him back because she loved him.

    Her husband, being the father of her children, played a large role because a person is more likely to let stuff go and give second chances if they have family in the equation. They started to see other people while they were married. It just made the situation even more difficult. She just reached her boiling point. A point where she was just tired of dealing with the same stuff over and over again.

    She was tired of taking him back over and over, doing the same stuff and getting no new results. She tells Eli that she stayed with her mother for a few months and she recently moved into her own place and she went back to school to continue her career as a nurse which she once dreamed about before life took her off course. Eli listened to her for hours. He was shocked and amazed by her story. Sometimes you simply cannot judge a book by its cover but read the pages in the book and they will tell you the true meaning of it all. Eli would have never thought that all of these things could have taken place.

These young women had being through so much yet she still managed to maintain a smile and raise her children by herself. Of course she made mistakes in the past but who hasn't. No one is perfect and everyone has their own unique story. Eli gained so much respect for her after listening to her story because she didn't hide what she had been through. She embraced it and had the mindset that either you love me for who I am or you can walk away not knowing my true value. Eli had come across a lot of women in his day but her story was by far the most appealing.

He tells her to come closer to him so he could wipe the tears away from her eyes. He was amazed that she would tell him that story knowing that most men would run away or view it as a red flag when she mentioned she was a stripper and had three kids. Eli tells her that he I respects a woman with some hurt to offer. He tells her that children should not be a problem if a man truly wants to get to know you. He will accept your kids as a part of you. She asks him, "How do you feel about me being with different men?" Eli replies, "It's shocking but I can't judge you for your past because I have a past myself and I had my share of different women. That's a part of growing." When a person is concerned about someone's past they still have some learning and maturing to do.

We have to learn to forgive and move on. Most people still have problems forgiving and moving on so they never let release the pain. Life is too short to allow old pain to stay with you. Most people think and process information and most people can't handle a woman saying she had sex with over 50 men even though the guy could have had sex with more women. America has a double standard when it comes to this. Male and female relations in cultures across the globe might suggest that women seek monogamy, whereas men aren't held to the same standards.

Men and women face the same problem: How to balance the desire for a close, intimate attachment with the desire for variety. Most women feel they can change a guy but a guy has to want to change and if he doesn't want to change then he will never change. It doesn't matter what she feels she can do. If a man, or woman, doesn't have the same characteristics they are looking for in a partner then it isn't fair to place the blame on the opposite sex! If you are looking for excitement and unpredictability, more than likely, your partner will be looking for the same traits in you.

No one can sustain a serious relationship that is always exciting or unpredictable. This can happen on many occasions, but a majority of life is not exciting and unpredictable, which is why this idea is controversial in itself. Relationships are built on trust and common interests. If you are male or female and are emotionally secure with whom you are then you will not need a person to challenge you or bring all the excitement into your life.

The notion that it is a man's job to be exciting, unpredictable, and fantastic in bed, at best is very shallow and egocentric. Some men are not attracted to women who expect them to do all the leading in a relationship, or challenge them. The good girl gone bad girl just listens as Eli expresses himself on the subject. She is very impressed because she sees his intellect and his desire to explain himself to her on every level.

She tells him to hold that thought so she can go to the kitchen to get another drink and check on the kids. He says no problem as he waits patiently for her to arrive but in the meantime he gets a text message from naïve good girl. She states that her boyfriend had blacked her eye and she doesn't know what to do because he has never hit her before. Eli tells her to calm down and call the police and that he will meet up with her tomorrow night so they can talk and come up with a solution. She says ok and he quickly put his phone back in his pocket. She comes back and asks him if he wants some chips or some refreshments. Eli tells her that he has lost his appetite. But he resumes talking about relationships and other situations in general.

He tells her that most healthy women like a man who is decisive, emotionally attentive, and good humored. However, most people, who are stable and emotionally mature, will not want a needy person who is looking for someone else to change an aspect or shortcoming in their life. If what you are looking for is someone to "Make your life exciting," you may need a shrink, more than you do a boyfriend. Relationships are about sharing responsibilities. No healthy person, male or female, would stay with a person who is doing all the leading or work to maintain it. A nice guy is always trying to be courteous to others and treat them kindly. They act like that because they are shy and lack confidence with girls. They jump into any crazy situation. They come off as being to needy because they are so accepting to anything. They should speak up more especially if they have a problem with the situation.

You don't want to seem desperate. You can't always be nice. The guy has to make the girl work and show she cares about him also. If you're a nice guy don't be afraid to do something new. For example, do something completely unexpected and crazy. People will be startled and amazed that they haven't noticed you before. Women and their female friends will ask, "Why can't I find a nice guy?" "The real problem is that men and women have a different meaning on what nice is. Some may view nice as boring, safe, needy, or whatever.

The thing is that they are all right because it is subjective. What one person thinks is boring another person may think is exciting. What men and women both need to keep in mind is trust and respect. Whether they are a 'bad boy' or 'nice guy' if they aren't trustworthy or respectful, then they are losers. Some guys seem to attract the crazy ones that want a responsible or successful man or someone to take care of them. People should focus on finding another half that compliments them and shares their success and failures.

The real trick is to figure out how to keep her interested after you let her know you care. When a woman is with a guy who is very easy to please, she doesn't feel a need to take the relationship any further. She doesn't have an interest in getting dressed up because he's happy regardless or even do little things for him. Women want someone they can look up to, someone they have to go out of their way to please. It's intriguing, it's fun, and it pushes them to be better. Challenge their ideas every once in a while. You don't have to be mean, but if you're so easy to get along with then a woman might feel that you're desperate and that she can be easily replaced by any girl.

If a woman can land a guy with high standards she feels like she has won the lottery. You're proud to be with the person you're with because you know you fought for them. And you know they must truly look up to you if "love" wasn't a word that was in their vocabulary before they met you and now it is. Women like nice guys but they aren't attracted to them. Nice guys often don't show the confidence or strength that women are attracted to.

You can't be quiet and timid around her in public. Just ask her out. Don't pour your heart into it. Don't act like you care about rejection. Don't be needy. Don't call her all the time. If you don't call, she'll call you anyway. Don't be a pushover. Don't do everything she wants, even if you want to do it. Tell her it has to be at 8:00 pm instead of 7:00 pm or Friday instead of Saturday. Don't give her money or gifts too often.

Limit it to holidays, anniversaries, and about 6 random days during the year when she doesn't expect it. Don't show your feelings too often. They want you to show them, but they want to work for it. Don't be clingy. You don't love her until you've dated her for at least a month or two. Don't act like it; don't say it. To sum it up, don't be too nice or too attached until the relationship is well established. Don't listen to anyone who tells you differently. Most women do want a nice guy; they just do not want a wimp or a push over. Only women that are emotionally or mentally unstable choose guys that aren't nice.

The problem is that many men think they are 'nice guys' when in fact, they are not or they are and have many other issues. If you date a guy and he has been dumped many times simply because he was a 'nice guy.' The truth is that he was a nice guy; but he also didn't shower often enough, he was too emotionally disconnected, and had horrendous manners! All the 'niceness' in the world couldn't fix some of his other flaws. If a guy that believes women won't date him because he is too nice, then odds are there are other issues.

Using the old "nice guys finish last" line is often a cop out and a way to avoid looking at what the real problem is. Is there an aspect of your personality that women have consistently complained about? Do you hear over and over that you don't talk enough, or you aren't social enough, or etc.? Listen to the common complaints and focus on that instead of the "nice guy" thing. Bad boys do have some appeal; however, most women really don't want a truly bad person. The person has to be a pretty good guy underneath it all.

The only reason that a woman would want a truly awful human being is that she herself has very low self-esteem. Women get turned on by how you are in bed, how confident you are, how open and attentive a man is in the bedroom, how he takes charge at times and not at others. He could be a total nerd Geek with a pocket protector and thick dork glasses but if he's confident and loving in the bedroom then that's what a woman would most likely prefer. The reason some women do not prefer "nice guys" is be- cause they think that if a guy is some type of bad boy that makes him a real man or that they can try to change him. I think that being a nice guy is the only way a real woman will actually respect you.

Some women sometimes don't know what they want or they have too many expectations of what they want a man to be for them. Nice guys may finish last but they'll be the first one a woman calls when they're having problems with their bad boy significant other. A nice guy makes it too easy and he may be too accepting. A relationship should feel like a struggle and without the struggle it might not seem worth holding on to or even getting involved in. But women also like a man with guts and the ability to stand his ground when necessary. It's a protection thing.

Women want to feel safe with a guy and know that he is not going to back down from a situation. Don't confuse this with a gangster. Bad boys present themselves to be fearless and often times can back it up. Women like a fearless, sensitive man! Men these days seem to lack backbone. Men, quit your whining and be a man. You're not a women! But in reality women prefer nice guys over bad boys. The only problem with most nice guys is that they become boring. Somehow it seems like the two traits are connected.

However there are nice guys out there who aren't boring and those are the ones with girlfriends. So for guys who think that they lost a girl because they were too nice, well that's not the case? If you assumed that the reason was because you were too nice, then you're really not looking hard enough at the relationship and you do not see what you really need to work on. Or if she told you that it's not working out because you're too nice, then she's lying to you to spare your feelings. In other words, if a guy is nice but also has a lot of other bad qualities, the niceness is not enough to hold the relationship together.

Some women do buy into the whole "bad boy" dating experience. Basically those kinds of guys provide short term excitement but turn out to be selfish, arrogant and only concerned with their own needs. But there are men who want "bad girls" as well for the same silly reasons. And there are the clingy, doormat or harasser types that call themselves "nice" but aren't at all. It's easier to blame problems on being too nice, too good looking, too intimidating instead of looking at the way you treat people.

Genuine good guys treat people the way they'd want to be treated. Some of these guys tend to be more introverted and less aggressive with women than the Mr. Showoffs so they may get overlooked initially, especially by females who wouldn't dream of making the first move and asking a guy out. But these are the guys that are worth the trouble of dating and often end up being taken by women who appreciate them. Different women have different tastes. If there is attraction and chemistry between two people, then 'nice' or 'bad' will not matter.

Acting as a 'nice' guy or a 'bad' boy will not get you women. As a matter of fact it won't get you anything. Being yourself however, will get you the person you're looking for. The more confidence a guy has the more he will try to show her how much he cares about her. Stay true to yourself in the process. It all depends on everything like culture and interests. Generally there are a lot of misconceptions about what a nice guy is. Simply put, most young women in their teens to even early 20's are impressionable and immature and some prefer the more dangerous type so she feels she is capable of loving, troubled young men that she can help overcome short comings.

Both female/male teens can either be shy and quiet or wild and carefree depending on the individual. Some young women don't get it! What is wrong with a guy having a cry or two over some- thing? It's healthy and it's a myth that men shouldn't cry to communicate their feelings. This does not make them weak, boring, or a wimp! Either the guy expresses himself and it's normal to communicate or you can guess and feel insecurity throughout your relationship. Some young women will spend hours in front of the mirror and obsess over the silliest things, but what they don't know about most guys is, they don't care if your hair is a little messy. You may have put on a couple of pounds.

They don't care! If you feel you need to "change" someone then they aren't the one for you. Never go into a relationship thinking you can, should, or will change someone. If they aren't who or what you want, then move on to someone who is. Nice does not equal wimp, but just the opposite. A nice guy is a man who is confident and strong, but not arrogant. He is comfortable with his masculinity without feeling the need to "prove" himself to anyone. He is also comfortable in being himself and doesn't try to pretend he doesn't have emotions or feelings. The bad guys though, tend to be self-centered, selfish, inconsiderate, and are also more likely to be unfaithful. They also tend to be more insecure, which is why they feel they need to be "bad" as though they are trying to "prove" themselves to others. It takes a real man to be a nice guy.

Now back to the passage they are both engaged in the conversation when suddenly they hear a loud noise. "Open this door!" It is her husband knocking on the door drunk and bloody. She quickly tells her husband to leave or she will call the police but he keeps on banging on the white lining of the door. He takes a rock and throws it against the door breaking the window glass. Again he yells, "Open this door now!" You could smell the drugs and alcohol on his breath. He pulls out a gun and begins to shoot in the air. With rage he says again "Open this door! We need to talk now!" This was the final straw for her. She quickly calls 911. She hears the kids crying screaming.

He finally snaps back to reality and leaves before the police get to her house. She goes into the kid's room to calm them down. She grabs her small kids and begins to comfort them grabbing them and hugging them tight but the small tears won't stop falling from the edges of their face. About an hour later the police finally arrive. She files a police report telling them the situation and what all occurred. She then goes in the other room with Eli. He is in shock. It is almost 2.45 in the morning and this took place. Eli is thinking to himself, "Does this goes on all the time?"

He tells her he has to leave because he has work at 11am and then gives her a huge hug grabbing her tightly as if he is draining her life away. She feels so loved in his arms. She feels safe and protected. She knows she probably scared him off with this situation so she gives him his space. He walks out the door and gets into his white CLK 500 convertible Benz and drives off without looking back.

The Options of the Chase

PROLOGUE

This chapter is called the OPTION of the chase because most people that are single and mingling have options and have people to choose from. A man that has a lot of different women interested in him is not likely to bother chasing after other women. He can weigh the pros and cons by picking and choosing between any young ladies that he feels is worth his effort and time. Some men fall in this category but not all. It's never good to generalize. I believe that if a man has more than enough women he is not going to put himself out there and risk rejection chasing a woman. A man knows whether a woman is casually kept or a keeper.

    My idea of a women that is casually kept is the women who is his friend with benefits or casual hook up or the on and off again ex-girlfriend. My idea of the keeper is a woman who is mature, has expectations, and is ready to build a relationship. In this case Eli is talking to three different women, that all have different personalities, and traits yet all of them are similar to a degree. They have gone about dealing with their individual situations differently because women might have similar stories and backgrounds but every woman handles her problems and situations differently. All of the women were caring in their own way and they each desired to be loved.

All had different things to offer good and bad. Let's break it down. Women in general have more options than the average guy. Women today have more options than ever before. A woman's option for a man have increased tremendously due to online dating and social networking sites where women are able to meet different types of men. Women that are objectively viewed as ugly or fat, those who could never get dates before now suddenly have more options than before.

Every woman has the opportunity to get laid because there is always at least one guy that is willing to have sex with her. That is the hardcore truth. Hot women are the cream of the crop, the crème de la crème of females. Guys want a piece of them because of their looks so a good looking woman has it very easy in today's world. Ironically, some hot women might not get as much attention because some guys don't have the guts to approach them. They already rule them "out of their league" because they are average or even insecure. Some good looking men don't even think they have a chance with them.

That is why I tell guys to approach hot women because you want to go for the gold. Show them that you are the better guy and add to their options. Don't deny yourself the opportunity even if they do have options there are a lot of older guys and old men that want to hook up with younger girls. Some aren't that picky with whom they try to hook up with. They all want a younger girl so they will try to have sex with them regardless of what they look like. Some guys will have sex with anything with two legs and a hole. These guys that don't care what the women looks like just want to run their number count before they get to old. It's sad but this is their goal and their lifelong mission. They are willing to have sex with any girl that will let them so the girls that let them only view them as an option, as a sex buddy, or a onetime lay.

As I stated earlier, every woman has the opportunity to get laid because there is always at least one guy that is willing to have sex with her. All you have to do is make yourself be that option but if you are able to make yourself stand out, you will be a better catch than all the rest.

The Options of the Chase

PART 1

The gold digger: She brings a lot to the table but she also brings a lot of pain and hurt as well. She is successful. She is intelligent. She has her own law firm, a nice big home, with some nice cars, and her sex game gets two thumbs up. Out of all the women, Eli feels she is the most successful and well-rounded career wise. Once he gets home from seeing the good girl, gone bad girl he just wants to clear his head. It had been a long week with all the different women.

    Eli needed to touch bases with the gold digger so they could hook up again. He gets a few hours of rest and gets ready to go to work that following morning. At work he just cannot get the stories the women have told him out of his head. He knows that he has to tell each one of them the truth about the other women because he doesn't want any hidden secrets. He wants to be honest as possible. He feels it is his obligation to be truthful because they opened up to him and gave him their story.

    Eli knows how hard it is to bring up the past and go down memory lane and open up bad memories you don't want to relive in your head. Later that day, he wanted to meet up with the gold digger and have lunch so they could talk. When his lunch break comes around he decides to call her. He asks if she is busy at the moment. She tells him that she has just left a client. He replies cool and asks her when she will be free. She says she will be free in a few hours and he quickly asks her if they can go out to lunch when he gets off work. She says sure. Eli can here a few of her coworkers in the background so he tells her he will shoot her a text message. She tells Eli that she will be waiting for him when he gets off.

The day goes on and finally the time comes. Eli shoots her a text asking if she is free at the moment and if so where she is located. She calls him soon after the text and says to meet her at Apple bee's so they can get some drinks. On his way to Applebee's, he receives a phone call from a strange number he does not recognize. Eli answers with caution, "Hello?" It was a male. The man tells Eli to leave his woman alone and then he hangs up. He tries calling the number again but he gets no answer.

He proceeds to his location and he pulls up seeing it is fairly crowded. There aren't too many people there. She calls him telling him where she is located. She says she is in the back where the bar is. Eli suggests that they sit somewhere more comfortable so they can talk. So they both order drinks. He gets a Jameson on the rocks and she just gets a sprite with light ice. Eli begins the conversation and asks her how her day was. She says, "It was stressful but it's better now because I'm with you." Eli smiles. He says, "My day was just a normal day at the office." He asks if she has been thinking about him. She says, "Why of course." Eli notices that she has changed her work clothes and put on something sexy to impress him.

He still has on his work attire which is a nice, navy blue, suit with a silver and blue navy trend tie. He asks her if she is talking to anyone at the moment. She replies, "Why? Why now with all the questions?" He tells her to calm down. Eli calmly states, "It was just a question. Do you want a sip of my drink to relax your nerves?" She smiles and apologizes. "I'm so sorry. Maybe I'm still tired and stressed from work." She shortly says, "I have a friend or two" and quickly gets off the subject. Eli notices her phone is going off a lot but he doesn't say much about it. She asks him the same question. "Are you talking to anyone?" He implies "Well, honestly I like you a lot and I feel you need to know the truth and that is why I wanted us to talk." Eli states that he talks to two other women and met them all in the same week.

He also tells her he feels that all of them have good hearts and have been through a lot in their life. She pauses and then she quickly gets upset, "What are you trying to do? Play me? I opened up to you about my life and my past and you're talking to other women? How dare you! You are just like all the rest of these dirty low down men. I hope you are happy. You got the goods and you man- aged to hurt me.

I thought you were different and I could possibly build something with you and trust you. I was a fool and never again will I let my guard down." She asks Eli if she should get tested then she throws her drink in his face. He is now drenched in Sprite. This showed him that he really meant a lot to her, other- wise her reaction would have not been so dramatic. Eli notices out of the corner of his right eye the good girl gone bad girl. She is with the man that had broken the glass in the window. Meanwhile the gold digger keeps yelling. Finally he tells her to shut up and listen.

You can hear the frustration in his tone of voice but he keeps calm, cool, and collected. "Yes, I met two other women. Yes, I think they are cool women but I'm not here to hurt you or sell you dreams. That's why I brought you here to tell you the truth before we go any further out of respect for you. Yes I'm single and I don't have a ring or a title so, therefore I can do what I want. I choose to treat you like a lady and be honest about the situation. I hope that we can act like two adults with some sense.

Allowing yourself to get mad is normal but look at both perspectives and allows your brain to at least break down the information correctly." She starts to calm down and realized it isn't her place to truly get mad at Eli. She doesn't belong to him and he is free to do anything he wants, but a part of her feels that she gave a piece of her to him. It was maybe because they had sexual intercourse. It made her feel he was hers. That's what great sex does especially when you're connecting with a person on all levels. The question is when is the right time to have sex? It's best to have sex with a person when you have a genuine connection with the person.

A mental connection goes far because you and the person have things in common. The mental connection or intellectual intimacy is the most overlooked form of intimacy. Yet, it is this closeness that usually first binds two people together. Granted, a man may be attracted by the physical appearance of a woman, but it is the mental connection developed through getting to know each other intellectually that first draws a couple to each other. Many couples feel that "spark" of excitement growing between them as they spend time conversing and becoming good friends with each other.

This process begins intellectually and quickly becomes emotional as well. It's nearly impossible to separate a couple's intellectual relationship from their emotional relationship. They're so tightly woven together that it's almost the same thing! Nevertheless, unless we continue to develop intimacy with our minds and intellect, our relationships become stale even sexually! You will always need an emotional connection. Talking to a person about your deepest de- sires, thoughts, and needs indicates an emotional connection.

You might feel this connection early, such as the first few dates. You engage about how things make you feel and your deepest aspirations for the future. You want this person to understand your feelings, even the things that make you angry. Some people express themselves through deep conversation and activities. When you feel an emotional attachment with a person, you feel comfortable around the person. You want to spend time together.

You pay close attention to the detail of this person when you spend time together and you create energy together. Your conversations go deep as you invite the other person to share more with you. However, you must leave some mystery between you so there continues to be an emotional sizzle. You draw closer through body language or by sharing affectionate gestures such as kisses and tight hugs. You cuddle up together when talking or watching a movie together. All of these physical signs are emotion- al connections. Having a physical connection goes much deeper than sex and touching. It's the small things like how a person smiles, their scent, or how their hair is done, etc. It's pretty much what the person desires or what they are attracted too. Spiritual connection is the most important because how can you build longevity if you don't have a spiritual backbone.

    A relationship has it highs and lows but the longest relationships are built with a spiritual connection because it's more than just a physical, mental even emotional spark. It's deeper. A person is truly connected with another human being by through the willingness to accept change and compromise. When first starting off you may not even find each other physically attractive. Maybe you passed each other with barely a thought on numerous occasions. Two people could be intellectually compatible or you may not think alike at all but when you tap into a much deeper connection which is spiritual growth, you get to know a person deeper. If you separated and never saw each other again, the connection would still remain.

    This can light the flames of physical love and it can cultivate mental love. You will develop mind, body, and spiritual connections that make the union complete and whole. Purely physical love will fizzle out and mental love can bring you into a rut. Both of which can potentially leave you unfulfilled long term. Spiritual growth gives you the kind of connection that covers all of the bases. Women have the hardest time trying to figure out the right time to have sex or open up to a guy but the answer is truly simple. When you have all of these components: mental connections, emotional connections, physical connections, and spiritual connections then you should be comfortable enough to allow him in and even have sex with him. It could take years.

It could take months or it could take days but when you reach this stage know that it is the right time. Sex can blind your judgment. You might overlook a lot of his flaws and enhance his good attributes in order to justify your reasons for sex with him. When you wait to have sex you gain access to actually getting a chance to get to know each other. You become more than just sex buddies or friends with benefits. Making the right decision on your own terms, at the right time, not only boosts your confidence and self-worth but it makes you feel more empowered in building something more.

Women wait until the emotional side of a relationship has been established to avoid a loveless string of sexual encounters that never lead to a relationship. An endless parade of men who disappear after sex is a heartbreaking existence for most women. Most women don't want a sexless relationship but neither do they want a loveless life. A lot of men want no strings attached to sex and will work just as hard at avoiding love while trying to bed as many women as they can.

Since most women aren't emotionally able to handle having sex and then being tossed aside they are advised to wait to see a man's intentions. Women are damned if they do and damned if they don't. Have sex too soon and you're considered too easy. Wait too long and the guy will get it somewhere else. While I wouldn't

THE GAME UNTOLD

advise a woman to have sex on the first date unless it's a connection like you have never seen before. I don't really think that having sex sooner rather than later makes a man any more or less likely to commit. A woman should have sex when she's comfortable with it. If it makes you feel more comfortable or secure to wait, then wait. If you can handle the consequences of having sex in an uncommitted relationship, then do that. But neither stance is going to make a man any more or any less likely to commit. If a man wants to be in a relationship, and really likes any particular woman then it won't matter to him if a woman has sex with him on date 2 or date 10.

If a man doesn't want a relationship or isn't so into the woman, waiting won't make him more relationship oriented but it might keep a woman who's dating him from getting more emotionally invested and more hurt. Since so many women have benefited from having options, I find the idea that contemporary sex "clearly favors" men a bit ludicrous. Unless, of course, you deny the fact that women have lower sex drives or might want to wait a bit before they marry. In the beginning of the dating chase, men are looking to get laid but they're also looking to make a connection if there is actually a spark to be lit.

Now, back to the passage, the "gold digger" tells Eli that she is sorry and she says that she just lost her cool. She says she really likes him and she respects him for telling her the truth because most guys wouldn't have told her anything and she would have had to find out the hard way. He bends over and wipes the pouring tears from around her eye lids and begins to hug her tight.

They begins to walk out and the "good girl gone bad girl" notices him walking out. Her husband stands up and begins to make gestures. It appears as if they are about get into a fight.

A few words are exchanged but then the gold digger pulls him away from the situation. She asks Eli if they can go to another location. He tells her that sounds like a good idea. "Would you like to go the river" Eli asks. She said sure. They trail one another to the river so they can talk. As they arrive to the river, there are a few rain drops falling out the sky but it is light so they proceed to walk alongside the river bank. Eli puts his arms around her and they begin to talk. He asks her what she wants and she replies, "I want you." Eli tells her, "It's too soon to want me. We haven't been knowing each other for a long period of time." He asks her if she believes in love at first sight. She replies, "I sure do." She starts telling him how he reminds her of her ex-husband back when he was sweet, spontaneous, and open and adventures.

Most guys run from a woman that comes on too strong and aggressive. That is a quick turn off for men. Men like for things to go as naturally as possible. They don't want to feel they are being pressured or forced to do anything that they are not sure about. Most women can't control their emotions and they come on too strong pushing a man away or making him not want to take it to the next level. The woman may actually be very sweet and caring but how she expresses her feelings is the key to building something successful. Eli actually likes the gold digger because she is very strong but he can't help thinking to himself that maybe she is too head strong. Then again maybe he needs that strong, emotional, woman next to him because he is very strong himself. They walk along the sidewalk of the river for about an hour enjoying each other's company. Eli soon tells her that he has to meet up with the naive good girl because she wants to talk to him.

    She looks at him with a mug on her face but she knows that she has to accept the reality. She respects the truth but she doesn't like the truth. She gives him a long tight hug and kisses him on the forehead. There is sadness upon her when she has to leave. She doesn't like the idea of sharing a man she sees as hers but she knows she doesn't have the title. She knows how rare it is to find a good man nowadays but she is content with the situation. If it is meant for them to be together then they will be together.

The Options of the Chase

PART 2

After leaving the gold digger he calls the naïve good girl. The phone rings and rings. She finally answers. She says she is at home and asks him if he wants to come over. He says "It's not a problem." Eli tells her he had just left being with the gold digger. She said, "What!?" He forgot he hadn't told her about the other women yet. He tells her that he will talk to her about it when he reaches her place and asks what her location is. She gives him her address. He searches for it on his GPS. He notices that she lives in a middle class environment.

    Eli arrives at her townhome. He knocks on her door. She comes to the door with shades on her face and he tells her, "It's not sunny. Take those off." There it was. She had a black and blue circle around both her eyes and a few bruises on her arm. Eli asks her what happened. She says that her boyfriend got mad because she walked in and caught him cheating, so she flipped out and starting crying and throwing stuff. The boyfriend told the other girl to leave and they began to argue and it became physical. She told him he would never hit her in the past and she was shocked when he placed his hands on her. She starts to cry. Eli doesn't want to tell her about the other women at the moment because she is already dealing with things. She really can't get mad about the other women because she has a boyfriend but just feels she eventually needs to know. She is very vulnerable and needs a shoulder to cry on because she can't believe her boyfriend cheated on her after all the years they had been together.

    A part of her knew he was cheating but she didn't want to believe it so she blocked it out of her memory bank. She didn't want to face the truth but then she caught him cheating face on. She allowed all the feelings she held back for years to just control her actions. She needed someone to comfort her and be there in a time of need. She felt Eli was the perfect candidate because she knew he had great advice and he was always sweet and respectful of her feelings. She tells him to hug her tight. Eli can't tell her no so he begins to hug her and tell her everything will be okay. She starts to come close to his neck and begins giving him soft kisses around the left corner of his neck.

    Eli tries to push her aside because he doesn't want to take advantage of her because he knows she is at an emotional state due to the situation that occurred. She whispers in his ear saying, "Make me feel better." She begins to grind on him. He knows she wants him but he doesn't want to take advantage of her, so he tells her he doesn't feel right. She continues rubbing on him and touching him and licking around his neck and he begins to feel a feeling in the middle of her legs. The temptations were at a great high. She begins to unzip her pants and the zipper gets stuck. She asks him to help her. Eli smiles and grabs her hands and tells her she should wait. She tells him no and says she wants it now and she rips his pants down and begins to give him oral sex. His eyes roll back. He cannot control his feelings anymore. Eli picks her up and takes her to the master bedroom. He begins to take her clothes off kissing her neck and rubbing against her spine. Her legs begin to shake as she waits for the rush of hormones to come down. Eli asked if she has a condom. She tells him to look beside the dresser in her boyfriend's pants. He thinks to him-self that they have to live together.

There is a possibility he could come to the apartment early after he gets off work. But instead of making him more cautious, this just creates a rush of hormones that enhance the thrill. Eli takes out the condom which is a gold magnum and he is struggling to get it open. I guess you can say he had anxiety because he didn't want the boyfriend to interrupt. He brings out a side of her that she never thought she had. Her boyfriend is the only guy she had ever been with.

He was her first everything but now she was having sex with the guy she met at the mall. She was in shock but she was addicted to his sex and how sweet he was. She didn't regret what she did. She felt that it was what she needed because her boyfriend had cheated on her. Why shouldn't she cheat on him? She tells Eli she wants more because she has never received an orgasm like that before. As hours pass they lay in each other's juices and begin to cuddle and talk about life in general. As they are laying down she starts to talk about her mother. She tells Eli about how she had a bad relationship with her mother. They were as opposite as two people can get at the same time. They were both very strong willed and independent, yet her mother was so hard on her growing up. She felt her big sister was treated better because her mother allowed her to do anything she wanted.

She felt her mother never listened to her and she could vent out to her grandmother more than her own mother. She wanted that close relationship with her mother but, every time she would come to her about a problem or situation, her mother would try to build an argument so she just distanced herself from her mother. She knew her mother loved her and cared about her a lot but she felt she was just too hard and never really allowed her to grow up and do things that other kids did. She felt she had to live up to her sister and but she was not her sister, she was her own person. Eli tells her she needs to repair the relationship with her mother because she will only get one.

He tells her it's never too late to build that relationship with her mother despite the misunderstanding when she was young. She tells him that she really doesn't talk to her mother because her pride doesn't allow her to. She tells him that her mother never really liked her current boyfriend but she just didn't want to hear her mother say, "I told you so." Eli tells her that a mother and daughter can become really close but they must always remember that they are not the same people. They're allowed to have different interests, goals, and ways of handling things. A daughter doesn't have to change her choices to please her mom and a mom doesn't have to change her opinions, either.

Mothers feel threatened and rejected when their

daughters are making different decisions. Daughters think that their mom disapprove of them and they get defensive which causes arguments so it's best to walk away because nothing will get done if everyone voices their own judgments and doesn't listen to what anyone else has to say. She tells Eli thanks and says that she will take that into consideration. Eli starts to tell her about the other women he had met all in the same week. She smiles and says she doesn't care about other women because she has a boyfriend already. She knows he is a nice catch so she assumed he was talking to someone. Eli is impressed.

Most women would have flipped out not being realistic about the situation. She tells him she really likes him and that he has been a gentleman from the very start and maybe she needs a fresh start from her control- ling abusive boyfriend but Eli doesn't want to be a rebound or a learning experience because she had never been with anyone different other than her boyfriend. She quickly tells him that he will not be the rebound and that she really and truly likes him. He just caught her at a rough period in her life and she wants to continue to talk to him, maybe even build something. She says that she is willing to be down for him.

Eli tells her that he will keep that in mind but he tells her it is getting late and he doesn't want to run into her boyfriend so he thinks it would be smart if he leaves early to avoid the potential conflict. Eli quickly puts his clothes on and proceeds to walk out the door. He sees the boyfriend pulling up with flowers and candy and he walks right pass the boyfriend as if he is a resident walking to his car and goes the other direction.

The Options of the Chase

PART 3

Eli goes to the local Walmart to grab some items and he runs into the "good girl gone bad girl" again. She doesn't notice him at first until he calls her and tells her he is behind her. She laughs and tells him not to scare her like that. She asks him what he is there for. He tells her that he is just getting a few items for his apartment. Eli tells her that he saw her with her man the other night. She quickly says, "I saw you with your woman the other night" he smiles and tells her that she was his friend. "I met her a week ago the same week I met you and someone else. We were just getting a bite because we both had a long day of work." Eli asks her a question. "Why were you with the guy that had just broke your windows?" She says, "He is the father of my kids and it's just hard to let someone go when your kids are saying they miss their dad. I told you it was a complicated situation." Eli tells her that he respects that but sometimes you have to know when to leave a chapter alone because the chapter has already ended.

    She says she agrees but when you have kids and you're a single mother you have to do what's best for your kids. She also needs the extra income because it is hard being a single mother. He told her that he understands the situation but not to allow the situation to make her do things that she knows deep within she knows she should not do. Eli tells her to look deeper into the scenario. "Your kid's father has too much baggage. It's good that you are looking for support and help for your kids but sometimes all support is not good help and support. What does he have to offer you other than more stress and a small amount of income? You have to look at the greater picture sometimes people can bring you down just by allowing them to eat your time away.

Time is everything and you don't want to invest the wrong time in the wrong person." She tells him she likes him and she respects his honesty and feedback. She tells him she feels she can trust him and share a greater connection with him. Eli tells her that he agree and he respects her testimony and the honesty. She smiles. She tells him she usually doesn't go deep into her past revealing painful memories but she felt she could vent out to him. She tells him they should go with the flow and when it's meant for them to hang out or possibly be together it will happen. "If it's not then I will just be a crazy lady you met that will forever be your friend." Eli laughs and tells her that she will forever be a friend, maybe more.

She tells Eli she has to get back to her crazy baby daddy because she doesn't want to hear his mouth. It's funny because she accepts the side female role. Maybe because she had her own problems and he was a breath of fresh air or maybe he was the side guy in her eyes. You can call her the other woman, the home wrecker, the mistress, the "thot"; but most will call her the side chick.

The side-chick is a complex individual but most people usually just write a side chick off as "thirsty" or "pathetic." Most times, it starts with just a flirty friendship. Both parties know where it will go but despite better judgment, they go forward. Innocent "friendships" and hang out sessions rapidly snowball into an affair. What keeps her engaged is that she is strongly desired. She is seen as danger, a thrill, and a taboo pleasure.

True, side-chicks can be heartless and there are many who have hidden agendas, like gold digging. But not all are like that. Sometimes, these things happen out of poor judgment. At this stage, she may be either fearful of catching feelings or she may start to feel guilty so she rationalizes: "If he really loves her then why is he coming home to me? Ha! I'm winning. I don't care. He's not my man anyway." These questions keep them in denial "He said he and his girl are about to break up. It's not really cheating. We have something special. It's so complicated! No one understands us but us." Things are getting hot and heavy.

She starts to fall for him. She is hoping that he'll choose her as his main squeeze. Phone calls are now being made earlier than midnight. She is texting during the hours she knows he is with the girlfriend/wife. She is now Instagraming couple photos and the demand for girlfriend treatment is rising. Some women have back up guys when they are younger. Backups provide some security, if the other guy doesn't work out, yet a backup holds you back from really searching for the best possible match. No one should want a backup guy. You should just enjoy being single until you meet the guy that's worth being with. When you use the term side chick and back up guy its shows your maturity level. When a woman or man has reached a level where they are tired of playing mind games and not really progressing or going anywhere, then you either will be single or focus on one person to build some type of chemistry with. Once you get older you won't have time to talk to all these different people. It grows old.

Hidden Secrets

CHAPTER 4

Older women desire love and financial stability along with long-term security and intimacy. These are the main components that a mature woman seeks. A younger woman goes through a stage where she is still learning and trying to find herself as a young woman. She might have countless amounts of boyfriends; most of these boyfriends might feel that she loves them or really likes them but she learns it comes with a lesson and every lesson might come at a different learning rate.

Most young women want to please their boyfriend, so, many times she sleeps with him if she feels loved or liked on a comfortable level. Younger women are attracted to older men because they believe that older men bring a mature mind frame, unlike most guys in their age bracket but younger women should realize that age doesn't define a person. The person can be much older than you and still be immature.

It depends on the maturity level and the respect he has for you because an older guy can still play and manipulate you. Some young women like "the outsider" (bad boy) because opposites attract but dealing with a bad boy can get you into many predicaments depending on the particular individual. When I use the term "boy" that is exactly what they are, boys. Boys are still in the learning process of finding themselves and trying to figure out who they really are as a person. Let's face it; most young guys cheat, experiment, and go through stages in their life to figure out what they want and in most cases a young lady's heart will get played with and broken based on that young man trying to find himself.

  Lady number 2, the "naive good girl", had a bad boy but she was too naïve to see because that's all she ever knew. Sometimes a person has to learn the hard way. Sometimes when you're so caught up in the moment you are blinded by the huge signs. Loving a person too much can make you lose sight of things that will bring you back to reality. We all go through a point where we have to be hurt or played to open our eyes and see the truth. That's exactly what was going on with the naïve good girl. It's sad that someone that innocent and sweet has to be exposed and eventually hurt deeply to realize she was silly in love.

  The fact of not knowing sometimes causes us to hurt deeply and it can alter personalities for the worst. This is how a good girl goes bad. She attempts to numb her feelings by being cold hearted, bitter, and not trusting anyone and sometimes not even trusting herself. Older women will reach a point where they are tired of the games which most men play because they still want to have their options. A man will only respect you if he knows for a fact you respect yourself. If he feels that there is room for you to accept the mind games then he will never stop playing them until you've reached your last straw. Then he will try to fix the situation only to keep you at the moment but once he feels that you're back on the same page again he will slowly go back to his old traditional ways.

Women seek and place a premium on a sense of intimacy and emotional closeness. Men pull away to feel anonymous, while women pull away because they feel negative emotions. Men need space from women, even if they love you. When a guy starts to back away, a woman may worry or panic that they are doing something wrong. A woman may think that his love has come to an end but the truth is women believe these things because when men take space, it means something is wrong but in reality all men want is their space. Men handle things far differently from women. Women have a larger capacity for emotional intimacy than men. Women strive for deeply connected relationships, not only with their men, but with their girlfriends, too.

A man loves to feel bonded with his lady but he also has a strong desire for independence. This is what makes him a man! It's not uncommon for a man to back away after being deeply connected to a woman. It's actually a good thing. The space allows him to come back to his sense of purpose so he can reengage with her in a solid way. A man will approach a woman ready for more love if she can respect his space. Know that his distance doesn't necessarily mean something is wrong; it's simply his way of feeling like a man again. Pride and manhood are everything to a man, this allows him to be more available for a deeper connection with you. Men feel competent by making women happy yet women feel competent by receiving from their men. Some women don't realize how important it is for a man to please his woman. A man derives great satisfaction by providing for and making his woman satisfied.

The problems are women often over function and over think the situation and doesn't allow space for a man to come forward to do things for her. Some women like cooking all the meals, controlling the schedule, and making sure everything is taken care of, but then there's not enough room for a man to be a man. This doesn't feel good to him; providing is actually what he wants to do! This, of course, infuriates women, sitting back and creating space for your man to come forward but a man feels competent by doing so.

A woman feels loved by being taken care of by her man. If you want a better relationship, give up some control and let a man start doing things for you. Men are more likely to orient to the world with their minds, while women are more likely to orient to the world with their hearts. Women can often feel like men don't get it. They truly don't understand the world of emotions, the way a woman does. Problem-solving makes him feel good! Logic makes him feel good! Being mind-oriented makes him want to fix it. It's just how he relates to the world in most cases, emotions as well, but they aren't fixable.

This is why when women have emotions it can feel so frustrating and scary to a man. The best thing a woman can do about this difference is respect it. Women, embrace your feelings. Your emotions come and go. Feelings aren't easily understood with the mind. Women you don't always have to explain your emotions to a man. The best way to communicate your feelings

is simply by feeling them. He may not get it, but this doesn't mean that he doesn't care nor does it mean that he doesn't want to help! What it means is he doesn't know what to do when you are having a strong emotional reaction. Remember, he wants to make you happy, so if there's something he can do, tell him what that is and he'll probably be very willing to help. Don't hold this against your man; just recognize that it's one of the differences between both parties.

No one ever appreciates that which comes easily to them. Women know this better than anyone. If they are "too easy," chances are the guy will leave them after they've had their conquest. The idea of playing hard to get makes the pursuer emotionally invest themselves in the outcome of their hunt. By making a woman work for your affections, you are getting her to commit to wanting to be with you.

Women place a lot of importance on how they look. It's for this reason that many of them get the male attention they do. Women understand that what you wear helps to get others to notice you. This isn't saying that all men want their wives to look like the latest supermodel though. What men really want is to know that their wives are making an effort to take care of themselves and not letting themselves go because it matters to them and the husband.

A husband appreciates the efforts their wives make to maintain their attractiveness. Many men appear to be unromantic, but it doesn't mean that they want to be that way! Men want to be romantic but they just doubt their ability to pull it off. They are plagued by internal hesitations, perceiving the risk of humiliation and failure as too high. Wives can do a great deal to increase their husbands' confidence in their romantic skills through encouragement and redefining what romance looks like.

This means that the vast majority of men respond to visual images when it comes to women and this doesn't just mean the guys with wandering eyes. Even the godliest husband cannot avoid noticing a woman who dresses in a way that draws attention to her body. Even if it is just a glance, these visual images are stored away in the male brain in a sort of "visual rolodex"; that will reappear without any warning. Men can choose whether to dwell on these images and memories or dismiss them but they can't control when these images appear. Men are often afraid that they aren't cutting it in life, not just at work but at home in their role as a husband. They may never vocalize this but inwardly they are secretly vulnerable. The antidote? Affirmation.

To men, affirmation from their wives is everything! If they don't receive this affirmation from their wives, they'll seek it elsewhere. When they receive regular and genuine affirmation from their wives not flattery, by the way, they become much more secure and confident in all areas of their lives. Everyone's natural response to this is probably, "Duh!" but that response is probably for the wrong rea- son. We primarily assume that men want more sex with their wives due to their physical "needs" but, surprisingly, the reason men want more sex is because of their strong need to be desired by their wives. Men simply need to be wanted. Regular, fulfilling sex is critical to a man's sense of feeling loved and desired.

When men feel their wives desire them sexually, it has a profound effect on the rest of their lives. It gives them an increasing sense of confidence and well-being that carries over into every other area of his life. The flipside of this coin also carries a profoundly negative affect. When a husband feels rejected sexually, he not only feels his wife is rejecting him physically, but that she is somehow rejecting his life as a husband, a provider, and a man. This is why making sex a priority in marriage is so incredibly important! Women are so in-tune with fashion, they really tend to notice how a guy dresses.

A man who understands how to cultivate his own appearance and looks good will get a lot of attention from women, not just because he looks nice but because he's communicating that he understands how important appearance is to them. Many guys suffer from the problem of having to "take what they can get." Women tend to get a lot of suitors coming their way so they can be a little bit pickier. When you know what you're looking for in a person, you're not only screening potential candidates, but you're making a very powerful statement as well.

You're showing that you're not desperate and that you are the one with the power because you are doing the judging and when you're the one with the power, you're the one who must be pursued. Emotions are what must be stimulated to make attraction work. Without emotion, attraction is impossible.

But too much of one's emotions is just as bad as a lack of emotion. Feeling good all the time or feeling bad all the time causes us to stray from the person we are with. When you alternate between hot and cold emotions, you create an emotional roller coaster that keeps things interesting and your partner interested. Women do this all the time. They will act very interested and attracted to you and make you feel good. Then, they'll act like you're not there and ignore you and make you feel bad.

This constant alternation of good and bad feelings keeps their partner invested in them and men can do this too. Women know that being sexual and using their sexuality is a powerful tool in attracting men. But men typically have no idea how to be sexual. Men equate sexuality with women because that's how they understand sex but men can be sexy too and being so will get women to become attracted just as easily as men are. The difference here is that in order for a man to be sexy, he must act manly.

He must show the best characteristics of what it is to be a man for the woman to get turned on. Using your sexuality as a man means being strong, being brave, being aggressive, and allowing your masculine energy to radiate from you. Being adventurous is different from doing what's unexpected. Adventure is about pushing boundaries and doing things that are new and outside your typical comfort zone. Adventurous women intrigue men.

They make them feel alive and those good feelings become associated with the girl. But it works both ways. An adventurous man will easily sweep a girl off her feet. He will make her feel alive and open up how she experiences the world around her. Doing what is not expected of you can create an air of excitement and uncertainty around you. It keeps people on their feet and attentive when around you. Of course, you shouldn't be comical when doing the unexpected, such as suddenly shouting out a curse word or something ridiculous like that.

Instead, you have to play against expectations. For instance, instead of complimenting a girl on her looks, compliment her on her intelligence. She probably does not get a lot of compliments like that and it will make you stand out. Taking her out on a creative date, instead of your typical dinner-and-a-movie is unexpected as well. Despite all the physical traits involved in attraction, having nothing but good looks can wear thin quickly.

This is why it's important to be interesting. Being interesting equates to having something to talk about that the person you are trying to attract can relate to. Being up to date on current events, pop culture, music, gossip, and any number of things can help a woman feel interested in spending time with you. In addition to knowing what to talk about, you also have to be able to listen and let the other person relate to you. After all, nothing is more interesting than someone who is interested in you. All too often, men ignore the sense of smell.

They don't bother to put on cologne or after-shave but women know that if you're going to attract someone you need to appeal to all the senses. Think about the perfumes women wear that drive you wild and you'll know just how important smelling good can be. Wearing good cologne around a woman can do wonders to make her aroused in your presence. Being the one pursued means that you have a certain amount of value to others. They want you, for some reason, and it's now their job to try and get you. In order for this to happen, you must place a certain value on yourself.

You must feel like you are worthy to be pursued by others and you must communicate this fact with your actions and attitude. Girls get lots of guys trying to impress them but it's the rare guy that they want to impress whom they wind up with. Women always want to know why men cheat. This is the big question. Men almost never cheat because of sex. Normally it happens because of some profound unmet needs. More often men are going to stay faithful in their marriages and be miserable for as long as they can take it.

When it does happen, it's not usually a "sex" thing. He's starving for something else. However, one thing I've learned about relationships is that problems within them are rarely one-sided. I'm not saying it doesn't happen and neither am I blaming the "victims" but a lot of adulteries in marriages fit into this category. Very few cases of infidelity involve a woman and man who were actively meeting one another's needs and one person just decided to stray out of the blue!

A man's need for respect and admiration will often contribute to him looking for it wherever he can find it - even if in the company of another woman. This is why, we the public, are often shocked at how "plain" some of the mistresses of prominent men look. We wonder to ourselves "Her? Really? He was willing to risk so much for her!?" When, in reality, often that woman has learned how to stroke that man's ego in some ways he sorely needed. If you cheat, you must believe this much: that fated love is a lie, and monogamous love is a deception. If you cheat, these two sentiments are your guiding light. Doesn't mean you're incapable of love, doesn't mean you don't want what love —or even marriage. Most men believe that it's perfectly fine to have a main woman and then other females on the side.

    As long as he can keep the two of them separate where there won't be any problems then he will continue to cheat because this is what his penis demands. What attracts men? Personality and a sense of humor, if a woman can make a man laugh that's really a great start and it's hard to ignore the personality that is warm and welcoming. Nothing is sexier than a woman who feels sufficiently good about herself enough to smile at the people she's interacting with, whether it's her friends, a baby or the waiter. She is not looking around for someone else to talk to or somewhere "better" to be. She has a glow. It's hard to describe this, but it's something you can just feel when you see it.

    You can tell that she's connected to her heart and is okay with sharing her love with the world. If a guy approached her and she wasn't interested, she would be honest, yet have respect and compassion for his courage to come up to talk to her. She gets attention without really trying. It boils down to finding someone who is of a similar cut of clothes as you. Most men that are strong like strong women. They have a voice and like to speak their mind. Power is the greatest aphrodisiac, and nothing is sexier than a woman who owns not rents her personal sense of power. Next, would be depth, this covers intellect, creativity, worldliness, values and emotional maturity.

    Men want a woman that has intensity. She has energy which is natural, sustainable tension, a key to battling eventual boredom. What turns most guys off is a bad attitude and closed minded women and a woman that is constantly intoxicated. Whether it's a bar, club, or a dinner party it just sends off the wrong signs. Another bad sign is if her body language is closed. If her arms are crossed, she's hunched over, her head is down, or her face is scowling, it's hardly going to make a man want to approach her. If you want to be approached, do your best to appear relaxed, open and inviting.

    Women should also make sure that they don't dress too sexy. It's one thing if she's showing some skin as part of an overall classy and confident outfit. It's another if she's doing it to get obvious attention from guys or as a way to outdo the other women. A woman needs to know how to attract with her body but also her brain and energy. No one wants a closed minded woman with a bad attitude or a woman who does not know how to carry herself as a lady. You don't realize how much a negative person drains from you until you've kicked them to the curb!

    Closed minded women think that know what they know and really could care less about a differing opinion. Closed mindedness and self-imposed ignorance are two bad tastes that were never made to go together. This is partly tied to appearance, truth be told. A woman that doesn't take good care of herself physically is more prone to be lacking in other areas of her life, too. There's a lot of fixing up to be done, in some cases. If a woman is fine being out of shape and not taking care of herself and has no other issues, that's okay, too.

However, I want a woman that cares about her wellbeing and physical health as much as I care about my own. It's as simple as that. How do you know when a person likes you? That a big question that most people would love to know. The way they communicate with you can say a lot about their real feelings toward you. Pay close attention to their tone and the level of attention they give you when you speak. Look out for their eye contact.

See if they are giving you their full attention. Watch to see if they break eye contact, occasionally but continue smiling because they feel shy around you. Watch to see if they give you full attention when they talk to you or if they are checking their phone and stopping to talk to other people. If so, then he or she may not be trying to impress you. But if they talk to you like you're the only person in the world, then they are engaged and you have their interest. See if they try to impress you. Do they tell stories that make them look macho, funny, or adventurous? If so, then they probably want to catch your eye. See if they talk more softly when they are around you.

This may be their way of telling you to lean in so you can get closer. If a person has you firmly planted in their friend zone, then they talk to you differently than they would if they were trying to impress you and make you see them as more than a friend. You should pay attention not only to how they talk to you, but to what they choose to talk about. See if they reveal personal information. If their opening up to you about trouble, with their friends or family, even their troubled past, then they value your opinion and like you. Because they would never feel the need to open up to you if it wasn't some type of comfort zone there.

Let's say a guy you're talking to or are cool with opens up to you about a new girl he likes, and then you may have a problem. This shows it's no true growth to build if he is bringing up other women but it could mean he is comfortable talking to you about any situation so maybe you can build something in the future. If you're talking to a person and they mention their childhood, that is a good sign because not everyone opens up to someone they don't see a true partnership with.

This is pretty private for most people, and if they open up about it, then they definitely are trying to get closer to you. See if they complement you. If they tell you that you look nice, or find subtle ways to let you know you're interesting or funny, then they may be falling for you. See if they tease you. If they feel comfortable enough around you to tease you, then they might like you. See if they try to be more refined around you. If you notice they're burping, cursing, and being generally a little bit gross around their peers but you find them never cursing and speaking in a measured and polite way around you, then they are trying to impress you.

Okay let's say if you're talking with a guy and both of you are very cool and you try to find where you stand, if he talks to you about other girls, it'll be for one of two reasons. Either he likes you and wants to make you jealous, or he just sees you as a friend and wants your advice. If he's always complaining about women he's dating or says, "None of them are what I'm looking for" then he may be hinting that you're the one. If he always asks you for romantic advice no matter who he's dating, then he may see you as a friend. If he says that you give the best advice, he may not be looking at you as more than a friend.

If he's always talking about his latest conquest but not asking for advice, he could just be showing off to win you over. But you have to be careful. You don't want to end up being just another number in his little black book. If he ever compares a girl to you unfavorably by saying something like, "She's cool, but she's not nearly as funny as you," then he's telling you he'd rather be dating you instead. But it can be game if you aren't studying or paying close attention to details because most guys run game and give you senseless compliments to get between your legs not caring anything about you.

Most women feel they know the game but at the end of the day, are left standing, hurting, and cold hearted because they have realized that they only thought they knew the game. Let's break it down. We're going to break it down so you know the difference between game and honesty. If he looks at you and tells you I'd rather date you than her, look at how he says it, listen to the voice tone and look at his facial reaction. Women, you have a gut feeling when something is wrong and something is right but most times you judge wrong therefore you pick the wrong guy. It goes deeper than your gut feeling and you have to know the person you are dealing with. Look at what they already told you about themselves. If he'd rather be dating you than her then why is he still with her and not with you? Also why is he telling you this? He is telling you this to see your reaction or to get your response to determine what light he truly wants to see you in.

Most guys cheat yet they don't have to cheat. They still do. They could have a good girl at home doing everything right but they still do her wrong. Let's say you're cool with a guy that is dating a young lady and he flirts every now and then. He is testing you to see how far he can go and if you give him any room he will take it and convince you or make you think he likes you, not her, to get what he wants at that moment but goes back to his girlfriend because there is a reason he hasn't left her yet.

The reason is that she is the only person he wants to be with but he also wants fun on the side because he hasn't fully accepted a real relationship. Most guys do this. It's sad but it's the truth. A person's body language can be a big factor in showing you if they want to get closer to you or if they just see you as a buddy. Notice how they sit next to you.

Do they always try to move closer until your knees touch or are they sitting miles away? Try to see if you can catch him stealing a glance in your direction. If you catch his eyes and he blushes and looks away, then he knows he has been caught! See if they always are looking for excuses to touch you. See if their body is directed towards you when they speak. Notice all of the things they do for you and think about what they mean. Do they bring you something when you're having an intense study session or get tickets for a movie you hinted that you want to see? If so, then they probably hang on to your every word and just want to make you happy.

You have to see if they do nice things for everyone. If so then they are just "Nice" and love giving rides and buying lunch for everyone in town, or do they do these things for only you? Remember, if they like you, then they treat you differently than everybody else. You have to ask yourself, what their purpose for doing the things they are doing is and do they do this for everybody. If so keep your feelings guarded because you don't want to be caught slipping and falling for someone that doesn't want you equally as much as you want them.

If you want answers sometimes it's best to just go to a person you are dealing with and tell them your situation so you have a clear understanding. See where the both of you stand so you can know if you need to fall back or keep it on a friendly level. It's good to at least confront the situation. Some people tend to leave their feelings inside even though they are gaining feelings for a person as times passes. On the other hand, you can you run them off because they feel you are coming on to strong.

They could like you but if you don't tell them how you are feeling then they will never know. They can't assume how you feel deep within. So before you get to that level, talk to the person you're dealing with so you can possibly save the connection between both of you and gain the feelings you seek in the future if it's meant for both of you to be together. This is when you're confident with the person. Try waiting around and reading the signs. It may be time to just tell them how you feel and ask if he feels the same way. They could be really shy and may be relieved that you're taking the initiative. Find some time to be alone with them. Make sure you don't ask them when their friends are looking over your shoulder. Be honest and open. Paying attention to how and how often you hang out and to when and where you hang out can give you great insight into whether they just wants to see you as a friend or if he wants all of your hang sessions to be more like dates.

    Here are some points to consider: Notice where you hang out. Do you see romantic locations or places where you see couples hanging out for date nights? If so, then he may want the same for you. If it's always just the two of you, then they may see you as crush material. But if their always inviting ten of their closest peers along, then they may see you just as another friend. Notice when you hang out. If you only see them once a month, then they may not be trying to spend more time with you. But if it feels like you haven't gone more than a day without seeing them recently, then yeah, they probably like you.

    Notice what you do when you hang out. Going out for drinks or a quick lunch is more meant for the friend zone, but going out for dinner or seeing a movie in the evening is a more than friend activity. Paying attention to how and how often you hang out and to when and where you hang out can give you great insight into whether he just wants to see you. Why do people lie? Well the bigger question is why do men lie? Let's do the break down. When- ever a relationship goes bad, it's almost always caused by fear, doubt, worry or insecurity that grows and festers until you feel overwhelmed by the whole ordeal and when this happen your fears and worries overdraft your confirmation that they're real or imaginary.

You stop enjoying the relationship for what it is and start craving validation and confirmation that it's the real deal and when you do this your relation or relationship goes downhill. It's like this; if you've showed yourself to be a woman who gets upset and dramatic when he tells you the truth, you're essentially training him to say what you want to hear to keep the peace. They will tell you small lies that later turn into big lies as both of you progress but men live in the mindset of wins and losses, victories and defeats.

What's the upside to being honest if it simply leads to a more difficult life with no perceived upside? If it makes since once he understands how to keep you happy he will give you a lie rather than tell you the truth because he knows you will get upset and will cause an argument. So women accept lies to make them content with the situation so they don't have to deal with the reality of the situation. It's crazy. Most women know the person they are dealing with lies but they never say anything to keep the peace.

Telling the small lie seems harmless enough and being honest will just cause drama, heartache and grief for both parties. Why would a man want to do it? I'm not advocating the behavior and I hold honesty as a high virtue for myself but part of looking at this requires us to be honest about human nature. Men and women want to make life easier for themselves, not harder. From one angle, you could almost look at this one as a compliment;

THE GAME UNTOLD

the guy is trying to impress you because he doesn't feel "good enough" to get you on his own. It's not a compliment though it's not only insecure behavior, but it also doesn't allow for a real foundation to be built for a relationship.

For a guy to be honest with you, he has to be secure enough in himself to know that you'll still want him if he's "real" with you. Why is it so hard for a guy to be with just one woman? Men are biologically hardwired to be attracted to many women. This is the same reason other mammals will mate with as many as possible to spread their DNA as far as they can, it's the ultimate success as a living being. A woman is hardwired to find the best mate possible and mate with him as many times as possible. You need to separate looks and desires from actual actions. Just because a man looks at other women, or even wants them sexually, doesn't mean he isn't being faithful.

It's when the line is crossed into him acting on those impulses or when they are being so overwhelming that he thinks about them more than he thinks about you. Then it becomes a problem because they are cheating emotionally. The average guy in the world has a main girl and side chick, and a jump off. Let's say you put 1,000 guys in one corner and one chick walks by. You are going see 1,000 heads go, 'Damn!'

They don't even know why they're doing it. It's just in their genes; they can't help it. Even if you're walking with your girl and you're holding her hand and you see a nice looking woman walk by and she's looking' at you like, 'Boy you better not look,' you are still going to want to look and you don't even know why that urge is there. Honestly, it boils down to maturity. When guys are younger, they are just living life and having fun even if they have to break a few hearts on their way to finding themselves and growing up into a mature man. It takes a while for a man to actually grow up unlike a woman.

A woman is willing to go through her phase of experimenting but it grows old and naturally a woman wants someone she can call her own so she gets tired of the thrill of the chase later. A man embraces it until he gets old enough to understand that there is more to life than having sex or being with different types of woman. Its fun at the moment but it never lasts long. Eventually a small amount of men grow up and become content with just one woman but a lot of men never become content and just live life and have babies everywhere.

A woman will experience much heartbreak and failure with unsuccessful relationships in her life shaping and changing her views and personality for the most part. You have to look at it like this. A man can only treat you how you allow him to. Most young guys hate the word commitment. It sends a chill in and out their body because they don't like the idea of being locked down and restricted. In some cases they can have a good girl and still mess up because they haven't come to the realization of being with one woman being with one woman.

It takes them a while to get to the point where they only need one woman to satisfy their needs. Most men struggle with this but it takes maturity and understanding to break this stigma of being just another guy that just wants sex and moving on to the next. What can make a man look at as you more than just some that he is having sex with? Well, first you have to look at the man's maturity level. Maturity level doesn't have an age because there are men that are older those acts like kids. It's the person that has gained experiences through life and uses their outcomes to grow for a better cause.

The first thing a man has to do is want to change because you can't force any man to change. He might give you the illusion that he is trying or he is putting in effort but he has to want to deep within. If he has doubts then you will get the same results. In a relationship, it takes communication, understanding, and patience and tough love. Both parties have to be willing to change as well as strive for a better cause in order to grow in the relationship.

Once a guy commits, he will lose the right to date other women. Most guys try to hold on to this right as long as they can, especially when they are not sure what they are looking for. "Committing" means "growing up" to some guys. A lot of guys don't want to grow up, delaying the process of growing up as long as possible. Commitment is a sign of maturity and some guys are simply too immature to commit.

It's hard for a guy to commit to one woman if he's got others on his mind. Imagine trying to commit if you had a couple of guys on your mind. This makes things confusing because you might like someone else but you like this person as well so your mind is at a standstill because you don't want to hurt anyone even though you are single and technically you are not obligated to anyone.

It's good to keep your options open because you don't want to put all your eggs in one basket but always let the people you are dealing with know upfront because you are not trying to hurt people, lead them on or sell dreams. You are simply trying to find the person that's best for you.

When you feel this person is best for you, through the time and effort of knowing every possibility of this person, then you drop your options and focus on this one person. Your goal is building not exploring. You explore when you have options and want to see who is best for you, but once you figure out who you want then, you drop everybody but tell them the truth. Why? Because you don't want to just stop talking to a person without a reason or purpose. Tell them why you did what you did and the reason why. Tell them because you found the person that is best for you.

They will have no choice but to respect this because if they care about you then they will want you to be happy. Never keep people on the side because it will always make things confusing and someone always ends up hurt in the end. In life, it's tough to balance love, family, work, etc. If there are things in his life that demand more attention than your love life then he will commit to the other stuff and deal with love when he can. People of all races have problems, terrible experiences, and mental downfalls. Sometimes it's good to be patient and put your foot in their shoes and analyze the situation.

People handle hurt and pain in different ways. For example, if he's had a bad experience with a past girlfriend or he's a child of divorce the unresolved pain in his past can prevent him from committing. Sometimes being patient can allow you to figure out the real reason why a person acts or does the things they do but not all people will wait for a person, to be on the same page as they are. If you are willing and see the true potential in a person then go for it but if you don't have time to invest then there are other fish in the sea ready to be caught. Committing involves risk.

You are essentially taking a plunge, and investing energy in the relationship. Some people feel that it's not worth a try unless they are 100% certain it will work out. But, you can never really be that sure of things and the unknown keeps some people from committing. If you are able to get the first guy of his group of friends to commit, I commend you. Most guys want to commit eventually but they don't want to be the first one and there is respect among guys for the last single guy in the group. Sadly, some guys are just out to conquest women.

Keep a close eye on things so you don't become a victim. Usually, if you have a gut feeling that this is the case, you are right. Most of the reasons a guy won't commit have to do with the guy. He may see you as a fun person to date but never think of you as someone he'd commit to in the end. It's tough to swallow when this is the situation but sometimes it's easy to resolve it in your mind this way and move on. If he's going to commit, let him come to that moment on his own.

If you continue to bring it up he may become bitter and annoyed at the whole thought of it. You'd rather him come to the decision to commit naturally on his own and not because he was pressured to do so anyway. Just think about how you feel when someone pressures you to commit. Any combination of these reasons contributes to a guy's reluctance to committing. One of the biggest factors in the success of a relationship is timing. If you're out of sync in a relationship with commitment then you may not be right for one another. What are the tools to make a guy commit? He needs to know that it's safe to tell you more.

    The more he tells you, the more committed he will become. For instance, suppose he tells you that he feels bad about not being a college graduate. Just listen and make clear that you love him as much as if he had a Ph.D. If he tells you that he's worried about losing his job, just listen and make clear that you will love him just as much if he does. This shows him that you are in his corner when he has a lot on his mind. Early in the relationship, avoid asking him resume questions. Look out for questions like, "How much do you make?" "Did you go to college?" "Where?" "Were you ever married?" "For how long?" "What do your parents do for a living?" These questions suggest that you are sizing him up and deciding if he is a good risk as a potential husband.

    A guy doesn't want to feel he's competing for a job he wants. It has to flow naturally and you have to equally engage. Remember, even if he turns out to be a millionaire, he needs to know that you liked him before you knew that fact. Ask instead what he feels about things, what he likes and dislikes. Because of his Masculine Pretense, your man is afraid to admit to anyone even himself, how much he needs you. But this isn't his fault. He hasn't had any practice at expressing his emotions freely. You can make him feel free to do so. And once again, the key is to ask for something. After a time, insist that your man tell you in so many words that he loves you. If your man repeatedly refuses to say that he loves you, if he never volunteers it, he isn't ready to commit to you and he certainly won't marry you.

Once he starts telling you repeatedly that he loves you, however, he will come to accept his love of you as part of life. Soon, he won't be able to imagine life without loving you. If you feel angry at the fact that he invites his buddies over at the last minute and doesn't pitch in with the preparations, don't make a habit of compliance. If you're not getting enough of what you want and find yourself feeling angry or depressed, it's not fair to you. Also, you will definitely communicate this and your man will move away from commitment. Your man wants you to want only him. He will be secretly flattered and will start to feel very secure if you demand this arrangement.

You're telling him that his sexual faithfulness is essential to you is, in effect, giving him the reassurance that you intend to be faithful to him. Even if your man protests or acts as if the request is silly, he will breathe a big sigh of relief and take one big step towards commitment. If the balance goes too far this way, he will wake up some mornings and ask himself, "What am I getting into?" He will want to swing the pendulum the other way, which will be bad news for you.

Early in the relationship, he may reaffirm his sense of maleness. Men often overspend on women they care for and then feel, "I can't afford this!" and run away. His Masculine Pretense makes it hard for him to admit that he's overextended. Maybe he can't afford the restaurants that he thinks you deserve at least not as often as he wants to take you out. It's easier for him to leave you and find a new woman than to disappoint you.

Make it simple for him to commit to you by letting him know that him spending his money is purely optional. Pick up the check yourself, sometimes, if you can. Or, every so often, suggest making dinner for him at home, or going to a movie instead of something fancy. It's the small things not the big things that you least expect that get the job done. Even rich guys feel this way. Offering to go halfway is sometimes a symbolic act on your part that will mean more than you can imagine to him. Playing hard to get might clinch the commitment deal.

Because of their Masculine pretense, men are crazy on the subject of loyalty. Most men, no matter what they say, are very insecure about their sexual desirability and about their appeal. Your man will be most likely to commit if he feels that you are completely loyal because you find him the most attractive man in the world. Don't flirt in front of him. Don't discuss past lovers even if he wants you to. Your anecdotes may turn him on for a while, but soon, he'll start doubting you. If you loved another man once and left him, maybe you'll leave him, too. And even worse, maybe you'll talk about him to some new lover.

Most of all, don't torture your man by playing hard to get and implying that he has to work for your love. He can hardly feel sexually desirable if he has to chase you and make big promises before you'll accept him as a lover. Once you two are really together, no surprises. If an old boyfriend calls, or you have lunch with a male friend, don't hesitate to tell him. You have the right to do what you want. Some guys carry their loyalty fears too far.

Things will be a lot less likely to get out of hand, jealousy wise, if you are upfront about your opposite sex friends right from the beginning. This is the problem with giving in to desire and having sex early on in a relationship. Once you've had sex, the relationship becomes solely about that if nothing else had time to develop. We all want sex and to be loved but when you don't take the time to build a proper foundation and become actual friends who don't have to share physical pleasures, your relationship only consists of the sex and everything else will pale by comparison so far as importance. "Why do we need to enjoy going out together when we already know we enjoy having sex together? Isn't that the better time?"

Compared with, if all you have together thus far is going out and getting to see and talk together, then that's the 'high water mark' but even better awaits. Strange yet true, but we've all been there: Sleeping with a seemingly great person whose motives we can't seem to figure out. Maybe they give mixed signals or no signals at all. Either way, something's in us makes us wonder if they're in it just for sex. Most people trust their gut, but maybe the gut isn't so trustworthy because it is wrapped up in insecurity. A person who is really into you will communicate regularly.

A person who is in it to sex, calls, texts, emails and pop overs only when they are feeling frisky and knows that you will indulge their desires. A sure sign he is in it for the sex only is when the person you're dealing with only reaches out to you after hours, also known as a "booty- call" hours. When the day is done and quite possibly last call has been shouted, the sex only person is remorseless, when it comes to leaving your texts not responded to for hour's even days and sometimes doesn't respond at all.

Unless of course you are reaching out to setup an appointment. You two speak one language Sex. And that's it. If you think hard about it, you may know everything about how they like "it" but you have no clue where their parents live, what they wanted to be when they grew up, the food that makes them gag, and if they have a middle name. There are lots of moans and groans, but no chatter about work, family, friends, and problems. A woman who presents herself as a sexual showpiece will be treated that way. Come to the table at the very beginning with more than just the ability to blow a person away in the bedroom. Blow away their mind too and that way he'll consider you relationship worthy.

You don't have to play like a virgin you just need to bring more to the table than what catches the eye. Sometimes you have to pay close attention to details and look at the signs in the beginning stages for example, he told you straight up that he doesn't want a girlfriend, doesn't have time for a girlfriend, can't deal with a girlfriend and just wants to have casual fun. It is up to you if you want to listen but remember, most guys don't want to deliver news that women don't want to hear unless they really mean it. Know who you are and be in charge of what you want from the beginning. Tell a person what you want and what you desire in the beginning therefore they can either say yes or no if you don't bring it to the table in the beginning then that's when the mind games begin to start. You can dismiss stuff earlier on if you pay close attention to details. These signs are useful indicators for both men and women to decide whether to take a relationship seriously or not. Do not be fooled that you can change him or her.

Another good indicator is that he will talk about his ex and how much he missed her or hated her. Either way you are just being used as a rebound until he or she gets his or her act together and decides to learn more about you. No point competing with a ghost. This is the way they attain intimacy. It is shallow and self-gratifying, but they can with cope with or risk being hurt if they open their hearts and are emotionally naked. It's safer to stay home and read a good book than to date these types of people unless you want a physical workout and can keep your emotions in check.

Hidden secrets, most people want to know things about a person that seem so hard to understand. My purpose of writing this book was to inform you about the game which in most cases will be untold or interpreted in a different format. It's the small details that people overlooked. Most women and men are similar with similar stories but they handle their situations differently. When people say they know the game yet they still wonder why things turn out the way they didn't expect them to turn out, then they truly don't know the game. It's not a game if you really think about it; it's just life and the many experiences you deal with. Most people have to learn from countless amounts of mistakes to understand the mistakes they are making and some others will never learn. They will continue to make the same mistakes over and over.

The Decisions

CHAPTER 4 – PROLOGUE

Eli knew he had to make a choice between the women because no woman would continue to stay with a man that has options. Most women will stay for so long until she gives up on the theory of being with a man that doesn't know what he desires truly. A woman can want to be with a man she really likes but after a while, as she is waiting she will lose sight and start to long for what she truly seeks which is completion. She might even start to open up to someone else that wants her attention and time.

Eventually every fairytale comes to an end and there is only so much a woman can withstand waiting on a guy that might never be hers in the end, so she will gradually move on. Some say don't waste your time hoping someone figures out you're a good catch. Others say true love waits for no one. The reality is when considering how long you should wait on a guy to make up his mind depends on several factors. Waiting or not waiting could depend on your situation, his situation, future plans, your age, and a host of other things that revolve around building something special.

The important thing is that you build a partnership with someone who is willing to work through the tough times and appreciate you. Keeping your options open makes it possible to have what you want, and it makes it easier for the person you have to give you what you want, because it completely changes your outlook and the "vibe'. Eli knew he had options but he didn't know which woman was best for him. All of the women had amazing stories and had been through a lot. There is a difference between having options and selling dreams. It's cool to have options.

Nothing's wrong when you are single and you are up front about the people you talk to in the beginning. Selling dreams on the other hand can cause damage and cause someone to be hurt waiting for answers. For example, if he tells you how amazing you are, and you feel like all your relationship dreams are finally going to come true but in reality he has no intention of being with you. A person should never assume until they know the actually facts because that's the quickest way to get hurt.

Earlier in the book, the gold digger assumed she was the only one and later got stung when she got the reality of Eli talking to other women. Most men will not dare tell you who they talk to but if someone respects your feelings then they respect you as a person. Next example, he doesn't call as often as he used to. He hesitates making plans with you or when he's with you, you sense he's not really there, and it hurts. Sometimes a guy can feel over powered and stuck so he can step away from the situation without ever really telling you so you end up with results of uncertainty and confusion.

The butterflies in your stomach are now replaced by a gut-wrenching tension. You're on edge, and you can only relax when he's with you but you never know exactly when that's going to be. Soon, you start analyzing his every move and talking about it relentlessly with your girlfriends. Sometimes you can over analyze and over think and you can make the situation worse than it really is.

The Decisions

CHAPTER 4 - PART 1

Let's break down the decision by breaking down the different women. The first woman is the gold digger. In the beginning, she came off so rude, so cold, and so bitter. He felt that all she wanted was his money when in the beginning all he wanted was a nut. It's funny because when he actually got to know her she was this bundle of joy hidden behind all this pain she haven't been able to release. You learn you can't help things that happened to you in the past but you can only focus on the task now. When a woman is hurt and fragile, it takes time for her to trust again and to open up and submit to a man because once you experience enough heartbreak and disappointments then it's hard to turn off the switch that you are so conditioned to feeling.

    Eli knew he had to take this in consideration because trust is everything and without trust then you're pretty much fighting a losing battle. But when you have options you can pick someone that doesn't have strong trust issues and is not as hurt and fragile, it will be easier building a bond with that person than a person that has their guard up. Some women will say if he likes me or if he actually wants to get to know me, then he is willing to be patient with me. This will allow me to let my guards down at my own rate yet most men that are already together and are a great catch already are not going to be patiently waiting to get a fair chance with a person based upon another guy destroying her trust level.

    Eli loved that the "gold digger was successful strong and jealous because that showed him she was dedicated and went after what she believed in but then again she was too strong at times and sometimes she allowed her emotions to overpower her logic. Eli knew this would be a problem in the future if he continued to build something with her. He also remembered that first night he picked her up. He noticed a tall man with a slim build leaving her house. He never said anything but he was curious about the strange man.

    He assumed it could have been one of the men that she would take from and used to get what she wanted. It was just too much to think about at the time. As Eli is in his apartment thinking about all the women and what they have to offer, he sees that he has a missed call from the gold digger, lady number 1. He quickly calls her back. The phone begins to ring and she answers. She says that she has to tell him something that could possibly stop them from talking.

    She says that she was offered a buyout deal from her firm allowing her to sell the business and move to New York to start a new firm. She asks Eli if he remembers that day when he picked her up. She refers back to the tall man that was leaving her house. "He is the same person that offered me the buyout deal of 100k for my location and a great location in New York free of charge. 'Eli immediately tells her congratulations. She then tells him that she turned down the offer because she was already well established and she was falling for this gentleman.

He looks at his phone in complete silence and tells her that he doesn't want to be the reason she turns down a great deal in New York. She then tells him that sometimes you just have to follow your heart because even though an opportunity like this doesn't come often, money can be easily replaced but love is hard to come by especially if its genuine love. Eli begins to tear up and asks himself if she overly emotional or if she a hopeless romantic going off instinct. He tells her to think about the decision. He tells her that just because they had a few good days together don't mean every day will be a good day. She quickly replies," I know you think I'm being overly emotional but I'm just tired of these different men I come by. I haven't felt this free in a while.

You give me this new energy, a new hope and an attitude about myself that's unbreakable. Sometimes you just have to follow your heart. I'm aware that I came off rude and like a gold digger at first impressions can be the lasting impression, but I know that good men don't come too often and in most cases I pushed them away with my first impression and my crazy attitude in the beginning but I'm not getting any younger and years are passing me by and who doesn't want to be happy? The game gets old once you have been playing it for so long. I don't want these men and their money. I can make my own money.

What I really want is someone to respect me and love me as a person. I want someone that I can build a future with. Is that too much to ask for? She explains to

Eli "I understand you have options. You're nice looking and you're successful. You're also sweet and you're honest, you didn't have to tell me about the other women and even though I over reacted about the situation I respected it. I was just being an average woman because I felt you were mines but I had to realize you aren't mine and I have to respect whatever choice you make. Sometimes being a nice looking successful woman is hard because all these guys try to use or see what they can get out the situation. Yes, we had sex on the first night.

Most people will look down upon it, but honestly I'm a grown woman and I can do as I please. Hell, I haven't had sex in over a year. I needed it and you were the perfect one to give it to. You respect my company, my body, and my mind because you listen to me. You gave me feedback. You were that voice that I longed for and needed to break me from this gold digger I was trying to become. That wasn't me deep within.

My situation made me become that but you released me from that wall, so I thank you. Sorry if I gave you a mouth full but I just had to get that off my heart and mind so whatever you decide to do, I can at least say I gave it my all and I respect you for freeing me from this old pain now I'm a new woman." Eli was in shock once again because she told him everything he needed to here at the time. She tells him she has to get off the phone because her sister is at the door and she doesn't want to be rude. He tells her it's no problem and they get off the phone shortly. Eli lies against his bed confused. He needs to get more answers and understanding from the other women so he calls the naive good girl, lady number 2.

The Decisions

CHAPTER 4 – PART 2

Eli calls her. The phone rings but she doesn't answer. He begins to text the good girl gone bad girl, lady number 3, asking her if she can meet somewhere around 7pm. She tells him she has to find a babysitter first but that sounds like a plan. He replies back and tells her to just let him know. Suddenly, he hears his phone ring. It's lady number 2, naive good girl. She begins to tell him that she has finally broken up with her boyfriend because she is just tired of dealing with the same stuff over and over again.

    They would break up and get back together, break up and get back together, she just had enough. She was at the point where she had to move on mentally and physically. She was just not into him anymore. She was blind no more she could see the light. She was upset. She felt used because she was so blind for so long. A guy she thought she loved really was a big lesson. The first person she thought about was her mother, which told her that the guy was no good. She gave this guy years of her life and now it was all for nothing.

    Eli tells her it wasn't for nothing because now she has learned from her choices and mistakes. She can move on and start a new and better chapter in her life. Eli tells her that to change, the first thing you have to do is stop thinking about what other people say or think about you. The only way to stop been naive, is to live your life as you like. The experience cannot be pretended or fabricated. It has to be learned. She tells him she is so tired that she is starting to view men all the same way and her heart is cold and bitter.

    She tells him that she will never put her trust in a guy again because she feels they will all try to play her and use her. She starts crying. She tells him she feels he is the only guy she can trust because he is always honest and open and always listening to her problems. Even when he knows she is blind, he had enough respect to watch her learn her lesson because it wasn't his place to jump in. She tells him she feels dirty because he had given her a STD which was chlamydia, a year ago but she forgave him because she didn't want to lose him.

    He took a deep breath when she said STD because he had recently had sex with her but she said a year ago so he knew that he was good. Eli takes his hand and rubs it against his forehead then lets out a sigh of relief. She asks him, "Why so guys lead women on? Why do guys cheat and hurt the people they're supposed to love? If he loved me like he was supposed to, then why would he put me through this pain and sorrow?" She screams out loud", I hate men!" Eli tells her to calm down and relax.

    He knows she is going through a heartbreak stage. He reassures her that, "If you are a good person, the universe wants to test your ability to be more; to be a great person. The things that we consider bad things are actually tests of character, allowing us to learn and develop beyond our current means. "Isn't it beautiful how a person can take a bad thing that has happened and evolve from it?" He tells her that in a bad situation something good always comes out of it. I have noticed that the moment a person diverges from the stages of grief, they end up not truly "getting over" someone or a situation.

You tend to want to avoid being in limbo, considering that it makes us feel trapped rather than free. One of the most essential things to remember is that when a person experiences a loss, we need to go through stages. When we understand our past and how it leads us to a point, we are able to use those points as improvements and we are able to create peace with the situation. Often, this will lead to a feeling of freedom and happiness. Being in denial is something that comes out of your subconscious to avoid pain.

What you can do is try to get some time on your own to be isolated from the situation. So you need to erase the memories you shared with this guy. Another thing is to be aware of the feelings you are experiencing and the reason why you are. Try to observe the situation from a more objective standpoint to get some clarity. It is a temporary reaction to deal with the pain and will come naturally to most. It is often a time when people insist that they are not broken up or refuse to let the other person break up with them.

It is alright to be upset and it is also alright to be angry. It is a way to show that you have been hurt and are upset. Try not to be angry at the world or everyone around you. Channel your anger for that person by possibly using your creative outlets or maybe you can even burn a picture of theirs. Take up boxing to get out some aggression or talk it out with your friends. Venting out is a good thing. I'm aware of what has happened and the pain is prevailing through the denial and isolation but instead of dealing with the losses with sadness, use anger as a dealing mechanism. It allows the frustration and need to fight what is happening out.

One of the better ways to go about it is to allow yourself to be truly and deeply sad. She replies, asking why she needs to be sad. She is not trying to be sad. She just wants this situation and everything to go away. Try to let yourself cry and feel it until you have no more tears left. Watch sad movies to activate the crying. A great way to relieve stresses and pent up emotions is to try to channel them through creative outlets. In my case that is poetry. I love writing thoughts down and letting them bleed on the paper. This is how I vent out but for you, your outlet could be drawing, painting, dancing, singing or numerous other things.

The moments when you realize that it is out of your hands and begin to let go, you can truly mourn because now you have accepted the truth. This is expressing your emotions instead of avoiding them. It will be difficult processing the raw emotions and it can be a stage that lasts for an undetermined time. The more important someone was to you, the harder it is to truly let go but the more you try to fight this, the longer it will take to get "over" someone. Since you are denying yourself the ability to grieve, your hurt and pain will continue. People often say things like "he or she is not worth my tears", which often comes from a place of hurt or anger. Crying and being melancholic isn't a sign of weak- ness. It is a sign that you are dealing with the hurt you have received by healing emotionally.

Acceptance can take years, depending on the person and their ability to process their emotions. Some people will insist one skipping the steps of getting over a heartache and heartbreak and jumping right back into a relationship but this will not help you deal with the remaining emotions of your previous heartaches and heartbreak. Being with someone new is not to be confused with acceptance. Instead, it will possibly leave you with unresolved emotions, possibly holding a torch for someone much longer than you would have liked.

She stops him and tells him thank you for everything. She tells Eli that he calmed her down and broke things down to her in a way that she could not see yet on her own because she was in too much pain to feel and think. She tells him that she doesn't want him to leave her life because she needs him and he is the only person she can vent out to and talk too.

Eli tells her he has a lot of things going on and he will try to be there to the best of his ability. She says that anything could help at this point. This sweet innocent young woman was now broken. He remembers when he met her outside the mall and she gave him butterflies. Now, she has become so cold and heartless. He then realizes that this is how so many women become bad girls. The men they invest their heart and trust in hurt them and make them never want to feel pain again but they all seek love deep within. It's amazing how you can love a person one day and hate them the next day Will you realize the truth? Eli tells her she needs time to herself but he will be there to pick her up and repair her because he wants to be there.

The Decisions

CHAPTER 4 – PART 3

Eli shortly gets off the phone with the naïve girl. A good bit of time has passed. It is now 6pm and he has to meet good girl gone bad girl. He texts her and tells her that he will be there shortly. She tells him to just meet her at the house. He asks if she is sure because he doesn't want to experience her crazy ex-husband breaking another window. She laughs and says that he is out with his brothers and I told him I had plans so he will be just fine sweetie.

Eli arrives at her house around 7:35. There she is at the door. It seem she has been standing there for a while waiting for him to arrive. He slowly gets out the car and gives her a huge hug grabbing her behind telling her he is sorry for being a few minutes late. She tells him that he better be sorry, with a smirk on her face. They enter the house. It is extremely silent. He asks where the kids are. She tells him a close friend is watching them for a few hours so we have the house to ourselves.

He starts to daydream for a second about the naive good girl and her situation and how she is turning into the good girl gone bad girl. He knows he has to be there for her because she will need the support and balance to get through this situation. Eli then comes back to reality. The good girl gone bad girl tells him that she thought she had lost him for a second. He tells her that he had a few things on his mind but nothing that he couldn't handle. She asks him if he is hungry. His response is "Yes, indeed." She says, "I felt I was obligated to cook for you since the last time you were over here the situation with my ex-husband happened.

 I just thought about something you were supposed to bring hot wings the other time. I guess I'll let you slide this go around but I cooked an hour ago. Do you like fried catfish, butter dinner rolls, collard greens, easy spaghetti with macaroni and cheese, cornbread, and dressing?" Eli says, "Yes, I love soul food! I'll definitely take a plate giving that it seems like you're trying to feed a small village." She smiles and says, "When you have three small kids that love to eat food is no factor especially when you get government help in other words EBT." She asks him if he wants her make his plate. "I didn't know what type of sodas you like so I just got a few." He tells her that was very thoughtful and sweet. He then asks for a peach drink with light ice.

 They finally begin to eat and just talk about everything. Eli asks if she and her ex-husband are still legally married. She tells him yes but says that they separated she only talk to him so he can be a part of his kid's life. "I didn't have a good upbringing. I want to at least give my kids an opportunity to have a mom and dad." Eli tells her that he can accept that and respect that. He then asks her if her husband ever tries to have sexual intercourse. She tells him yes. "All the time but I haven't had sex with my ex-husband in over a year now. Sometimes when he drinks he turn into another person. I cannot deal with that any longer.

I have out grown the situation and we only communicate out of respect for my three kids. I have recently gotten saved and given my life to the lord and I am a proud member of the local church in the inner city. I admit I have a crazy past. I have been through so much from being abused to even being raped. I sold my soul, self-respect, and pride for money. I have been through hell and back but now it's time to see the light. I'm not saying I'm perfect because every now and then I think about the past but I have to think about my kids and their future.

Most men can't handle my story. It's fine and I understand but if God can forgive me and my faults why can't men do the same? I have shed my last tears. I'm tired of hurting and not loving myself. It is time for a change and a spiritual breakthrough. When you find a deeper satisfaction in your soul through a relationship with Christ, then you will really start to feel comfortable in a relationship but like any meaningful relationship, it requires work, time, effort, patience and persistence. Finding your soul mate is not the primary reason you were created.

The main reason is even better because it involves a loving relationship with your Creator. The whole soul mate thing is just a bonus. The first priority is that you grow close to the Lord. You end up way ahead and you reach goals you didn't even know could be reached back when you were trying to solve and figure out life and your purpose. By loving the lord first and foremost, you are positioning yourself to receive God's plan for your life.

Whatever course that takes, you can trust Him to meet the needs of your soul and the longings of your heart. I feel like my life and things that happened to me were for a reason. I have learned from my situation and grown into better person and mother I recently got accept in nursing school which was one of my main goals before I got off track.

    Now that I have a better relationship with God everything is starting to come together. I remember when I first met you at the local Kroger. You probably judged me based on my experiences. I thought you were like most men and some never take time to know a person's story before they make the assumption and judgment. I guess that's human nature but for some reason you were different you could have tried to have sex with me but you took time to listen to my story and give me feedback. Most men would have reacted on judged without even trying to understand.

    This showed me you were not the average man but that you are truly one of a kind. You were even honest with me about the other women you were dealing with and most men would have never said a word. When you told me about the situation I was calm and collected because it wasn't my place to get upset." Eli was impressed. Out of all the women, she always surprised him the most but he had to think to himself. Could he really build a future with a lady with kids? Her story and her past wasn't the problem. She came with a lot of baggage but he knew she was a good woman but could he really see himself with her?

Concluding Thoughts

Every person has similar problems, similar situations. Yet every person is different in their own unique way. Two individuals can share the same story but handle the situation differently. The gold digger, the naive good girl, and the good girl gone bad girl are the characters in the book. But there is more depth to each character than their names imply. A person reading this may be able to relate to one character more than another or maybe they might have bits and pieces of each. That's why I simply gave them titles instead of names.

People always say it's hard to find someone that has all the attributes you desire, but you have to be realistic. Not everyone is going to possess all the qualities that you seek in a potential candidate. I always felt that if a person has most of what you desire and there good qualities outweigh their bad ones then this is the person for you. In any relationship you are going to have problems and disagreements, but ask yourself this, are you willing to work the problem out or argue till both parties are upset and holding grudges that they are not willing to admit to? When this occurs nothing gets resolved and this small thing can make a large impact on the future. Ask yourself this, what person am I willing to go through hell and back with at the end of the day?

People are most likely always going to have misunderstandings or disagreements. I wrote this book because most people want to know the game, and what I mean by game is how to not be played or go into a situation blindly without knowing what they are getting themselves self into. So if you could skip, the chase, the exchange and the thrill of the chase, then you could save yourself a lot of time and possibly a heartbreak. I used the scenario of a man that was not so average and very diverse, meeting three different women with three different backgrounds and stories.

He analyzed them in the beginning, dissected them, studied them, and gave them feedback to fix their situations and problems, while also allowing the reader to learn the game, which is untold. The reader will make a choice based on what they will learn throughout the book eventually deciding who Eli should choose. He may choose the gold digger, the naive good girl or good girl gone bad girl or he may not choose any of them. It's not my call to choose for you. I have simply given you the information and you must choose based on what you feel is right. Many people inspired me to write this book. The book came from a lot of concepts and creative ideas I have developed over the years. I have used my vivid imagination and my own personal relationships as well as those of my friends and family in order to write this book.

About the Author

My name is Tyrus Rashod Brown (Tucker) but most people know me by my nickname, Tuck. I was the guy that had to get a GED and wasn't able to complete high school with all of my peers but now I have two college degrees. One of my degrees is from the University of Memphis and I also have a degree from Southwest Community College. I now have my real estate license as well. At one point I was homeless with no job and no place to stay. I had no car and no real family support. I asked myself, what I would do with my life. I watched my mother Debra R. Tucker (Smith) struggle while raising five kids. Growing up without a father in my life was hard.

    I had dreams much larger than my situation. I was exposed to everything from gangs, drugs sex, murder, jail, etc. You name it I've seen it. I've lived it. A lot of people told me that I wouldn't make it but I knew that I would prove everybody wrong. I started with nothing. I moved all the time from house to house. I had lived all around Memphis. I had been in 39 different locations before the age of 16. Something had to change, I felt as though I was out here in this big world all alone struggling and being talked about. My family didn't have the funds that everyone else's had but one thing I had was vision. I also had determination. This relentless effort was a will of force that created a burning desire inside me that gave me the strength to make it against any obstacle.

    I stopped complaining and started making things happen. I stopped making excuses and starting making moves. I left my past in the past started focusing on what I could do now and started looking toward my future. It took many failures to see a few big successes. I never gave up because I wanted to help my family. I have come a long way since those times but still have a long way to go because my dreams and goals are so much larger than those of the average mind. I've already accomplished so much at such a young age.

    I'm not just another black statistic. I notice that there are more women than men in college. I fear for my fellow black brothers. My long term goal is to help other black men elevate their minds, to inspire them and to shape them into the men I know they can be. I seek to change our generation's curse which has enslaved us mentally. One day we will shatter the invisible boundaries that we don't talk about but we all still deal with. Once this is done, our young men can see their true potential.

www.ingramcontent.com/pod-product-compliance
Lightning Source LLC
Chambersburg PA
CBHW020357170426
43200CB00005B/200